GLOBALVIEWPOINTS

# The Arab-Israeli Conflict

# Other Books of Related Interest:

**At Issue Series**

Weapons of War

**Current Controveries Series**

Iran

The Iranian Green Movement

The Middle East

**Global Viewpoints Series**

Discrimination

Human Rights

**Opposing Viewpoints Series**

America's Global Influence

Extremism

Israel

The Taliban

United Nations

GLOBALVIEWPOINTS

# The Arab-Israeli Conflict

*Noah Berlatsky, Book Editor*

**GREENHAVEN PRESS**
*A part of Gale, Cengage Learning*

GALE
CENGAGE Learning

Detroit • New York • San Francisco • New Haven, Conn • Waterville, Maine • London

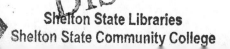

Elizabeth Des Chenes, *Managing Editor*

© 2012 Greenhaven Press, a part of Gale, Cengage Learning

Gale and Greenhaven Press are registered trademarks used herein under license.

*For more information, contact:*
Greenhaven Press
27500 Drake Rd.
Farmington Hills, MI 48331-3535
Or you can visit our Internet site at gale.cengage.com

For product information and technology assistance, contact us at

Gale Customer Support, 1-800-877-4253
For permission to use material from this text or product, submit all requests online at www.cengage.com/permissions

Further permissions questions can be emailed to permissionrequest@cengage.com

Articles in Greenhaven Press anthologies are often edited for length to meet page requirements. In addition, original titles of these works are changed to clearly present the main thesis and to explicitly indicate the author's opinion. Every effort is made to ensure that Greenhaven Press accurately reflects the original intent of the authors. Every effort has been made to trace the owners of copyrighted material.

Cover image copyright © Ahmad Gharabli/AFP/Getty Images.

LIBRARY OF CONGRESS CATALOGING-IN-PUBLICATION DATA

The Arab-Israeli conflict / Noah Berlatsky, book editor.
p. cm. -- (Global viewpoints)
Summary: "Global Viewpoints: The Arab-Israeli Conflict: Regional Issues and the Arab-Israeli Conflict; Israel and the Gaza Strip; Israel and the West Bank; International Involvement in the Arab-Israeli Conflict"-- Provided by publisher.
Includes bibliographical references and index.
ISBN 978-0-7377-5644-9 (hardback) -- ISBN 978-0-7377-5645-6 (pbk.)
1. Arab-Israeli conflict--1993- I. Berlatsky, Noah.
DS119.76.A722 2012
956.05'4--dc23
2011036992

Printed in Mexico
1 2 3 4 5 6 7 16 15 14 13 12

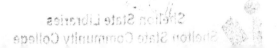

# Contents

In November 2007 Israel bombed and destroyed a nuclear plant in Syria. This appears to have destroyed Syria's nuclear capabilities but has not effectively dissuaded Iran.

# Chapter 2: Israel and the Gaza Strip

Israel did not target civilians during the 2008–2009 Gaza war. Evidence suggests therefore that Israel was not guilty of war crimes. Hamas, on the other hand, intentionally perpetrated war crimes.

# Chapter 3: Israel and the West Bank

Despite Arab attempts to discourage their settlement on the West Bank, Israel believes their communities to be legitimate and will not let fear keep them from defending their settlements in what they consider their homeland.

# Chapter 4: International Involvement in the Arab-Israeli Conflict

The European Union has long been closely involved in the Middle Eastern peace process. Its involvement would be more effective if it delinked the Palestinian peace process from other regional issues.

# Foreword

> "The problems of all of humanity can
> only be solved by all of humanity."
> —Swiss author Friedrich Dürrenmatt

Global interdependence has become an undeniable reality. Mass media and technology have increased worldwide access to information and created a society of global citizens. Understanding and navigating this global community is a challenge, requiring a high degree of information literacy and a new level of learning sophistication.

Building on the success of its flagship series, Opposing Viewpoints, Greenhaven Press has created the Global Viewpoints series to examine a broad range of current, often controversial topics of worldwide importance from a variety of international perspectives. Providing students and other readers with the information they need to explore global connections and think critically about worldwide implications, each Global Viewpoints volume offers a panoramic view of a topic of widespread significance.

Drugs, famine, immigration—a broad, international treatment is essential to do justice to social, environmental, health, and political issues such as these. Junior high, high school, and early college students, as well as general readers, can all use Global Viewpoints anthologies to discern the complexities relating to each issue. Readers will be able to examine unique national perspectives while, at the same time, appreciating the interconnectedness that global priorities bring to all nations and cultures.

Material in each volume is selected from a diverse range of sources, including journals, magazines, newspapers, nonfiction books, speeches, government documents, pamphlets, organization newsletters, and position papers. Global Viewpoints is truly global, with material drawn primarily from international sources available in English and secondarily from US sources with extensive international coverage.

Features of each volume in the Global Viewpoints series include:

- An **annotated table of contents** that provides a brief summary of each essay in the volume, including the name of the country or area covered in the essay.

- An **introduction** specific to the volume topic.

- A **world map** to help readers locate the countries or areas covered in the essays.

- For each viewpoint, an **introduction** that contains notes about the author and source of the viewpoint explains why material from the specific country is being presented, summarizes the main points of the viewpoint, and offers three **guided reading questions** to aid in understanding and comprehension.

- **For further discussion** questions that promote critical thinking by asking the reader to compare and contrast aspects of the viewpoints or draw conclusions about perspectives and arguments.

- A worldwide list of **organizations to contact** for readers seeking additional information.

- A **periodical bibliography** for each chapter and a **bibliography of books** on the volume topic to aid in further research.

- A comprehensive **subject index** to offer access to people, places, events, and subjects cited in the text, with the countries covered in the viewpoints highlighted.

Global Viewpoints is designed for a broad spectrum of readers who want to learn more about current events, history, political science, government, international relations, economics, environmental science, world cultures, and sociology— students doing research for class assignments or debates, teachers and faculty seeking to supplement course materials, and others wanting to understand current issues better. By presenting how people in various countries perceive the root causes, current consequences, and proposed solutions to worldwide challenges, Global Viewpoints volumes offer readers opportunities to enhance their global awareness and their knowledge of cultures worldwide.

# Introduction

China's position in relation to the Arab/Israeli conflict has undergone substantial changes in the last sixty years.

Israel was "the first country in the Middle East and one of the first in the world" to recognize the Communist government of the People's Republic of China following its establishment in 1949, according to Cnaan Liphshiz in a September 25, 2009, article in *Haaretz*. However, as relations between China and the West became more and more strained, China's relations with Israel also soured. From the mid-1950s, "China began to regard Israel as an instrument of Western imperialism for exerting pressure on the Arab countries and for maintaining tension in the Middle East," according to Yitzhak Shichor's *The Middle East in China's Foreign Policy, 1949–1977*. China came to believe, according to Shichor, that reducing Western influence in the Middle East was vital for reducing Western influence worldwide. Partially as a result, China tended to side with Arab nations in the Arab/Israeli conflict.

One of the most important ways in which China supported the Arabs in the 1980s and 1990s was with arms sales. "At this time, Arab states were looking to obtain weapons to bolster their defensive capabilities against new threats, while China wanted to expand its export market as a source of revenue for its military and civilian modernization programs," explains Mohamed Bin Huwaidin's article "China in the Middle East: Perspectives from the Arab World," reprinted on the Arab Insight website. For instance, the Iran-Iraq war of the 1980s led Saudi Arabia to strengthen its security, mostly by purchasing Chinese weapons.

As the Cold War came to a close with the collapse of the Soviet Union in the late 1980s, and as China began to prioritize economic expansion, its relations with the West have improved. Along with that improvement has come a thawing of relations with Israel. China finally officially established diplomatic relations with Israel in 1992. Though initial trade was "modest . . . the bilateral trade between the two countries has already reached 6.7 billion US$ in 2010," according to an article posted on the website of Israel's Trade Mission to China.

At the same time as its trade with Israel has grown, China has maintained important trade relations with Arab nations. In particular, China's rapid growth has made it very interested in Middle East oil. According to Mohamed Bin Huwaidin, "China alone is currently responsible for about 38 percent of the total global growth in demand for oil. With the world's largest proven oil reserves in the Middle East and North Africa, China's energy needs made reinvigorated relations with Middle Eastern states inevitable."

Because of its close ties with Israel and with Arab nations, and because of its growing influence worldwide, many commentators have expressed hope that China may be able to play a central role in resolving the Arab/Israeli conflict. For instance, Robert Dreyfuss, writing at his blog on the website of the *Nation*, hopes that China's close relations with Iran and Saudi Arabia may help to resolve tensions in the region. Dreyfuss approvingly quotes analyst Ken Pollack who said that "China has exactly the same interests as the United States in the Middle East"—that is, both China and the United States want stability so that oil will be readily available at a reasonable price. "You've got to let [China] in," Pollack concluded. "You've got to make them our partner."

On the other hand, some see the growth of China as a cause of greater rivalry and tension between east and west over the Middle East. For example, John Chan in a January 11, 2010, article on the Global Research website, argues that "the US-led wars in Iraq and Afghanistan, its proxy war in Pakistan and threats against Iran are driven by Washington's determination to dominate the key strategic regions of the Middle East and central Asia, to the exclusion of its rivals, especially China." Similarly, in an article for the Institute for the Analysis of Global Security, Gal Luft notes that while "in the short term, China recognizes that its energy security is increasingly dependent on cooperation with the U.S.," there is also a "feeling among many Chinese leaders that the U.S. seeks to dominate the Persian Gulf in order to exercise control over its energy resources and that it tries to contain China's aspirations in the region. The U.S. is therefore considered a major threat to China's long-term energy security."

Whatever its tensions with the West, China has urged both Arabs and Israelis to move toward peace in the Middle East. For instance, a March 23, 2011, article on Xinhuanet.com reporting on Chinese Middle East envoy Wu Sike's efforts to encourage peace, notes that Wu had called for an end to settlement expansion and hoped for, as the article says, "all relevant parties to create appropriate conditions and restart the stalled Middle East peace process as soon as possible."

But whatever may happen in the future, Mohamed Bin Huwaidin suggests that China is not yet ready to take a central role in Middle East negotiations. "Despite international appraisals of China's ascent," Huwaidin says, "China still categorizes itself as a regional power out of fear that it will jeopardize its rise by alarming other international powers." Still, while China may not be as involved now as it might be in the future, Jon Alterman, writing in an August 7, 2008, post at

*Middle East Strategy at Harvard,* notes that "it is hard to imagine a future in the Middle East in which China does not play a more substantial role."

The remainder of this book looks at the Arab-Israeli conflict from a global perspective in chapters titled Regional Issues and the Arab/Israeli Conflict, Israel and the Gaza Strip, Israel and the West Bank, and International Involvement in the Arab-Israeli Conflict. The Middle East is one of the most important and most volatile regions on earth, and its tensions generate discussion and viewpoints from commentators all over the world.

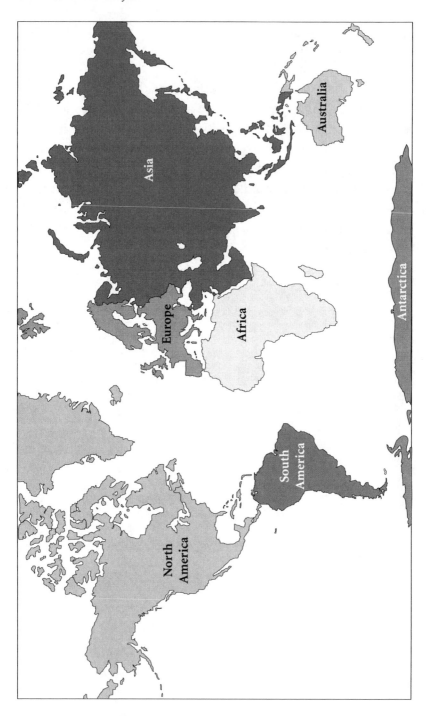

GLOBAL VIEWPOINTS

## CHAPTER 1

# Regional Issues and the Arab-Israeli Conflict

# The Unrest in the Middle East May Isolate Israel

## David Horovitz

*David Horovitz is the editor in chief of the Israeli newspaper the Jerusalem Post. In the following viewpoint, he argues that the instability in the Middle East represents a serious danger to Israel. He says that the Israel-Egypt peace treaty of 1979 has been a defining element of Israel's diplomatic and security strategy. Now, in 2011, as Egypt experiences major street protests and the toppling of the regime of Hosni Mubarak, Horovitz worries that the peace agreement may be voided. Horovitz is concerned that Mubarak's government will be replaced with a radical Islamic government like that of Iran, which is hostile to Israel.*

As you read, consider the following questions:

1. What events does Horovitz point to in order to show that the Middle East is in ferment as he writes?

2. What does Horovitz say is preventing Israel from making territorial compromises in the cause of peace?

3. According to Horovitz, what vital regional alliance other than Egypt has slipped away from Israel?

The Middle East is in ferment at the moment [February 1, 2011]—but despite the general excitement, the outcome could be a grim one for Israel, and for the West more generally.

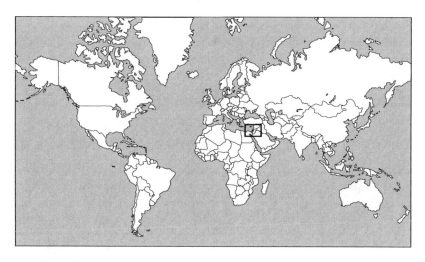

# Egypt Totters

In the past few weeks, we have seen a president ousted in Tunisia. We've seen protests in Yemen. We've seen Iran essentially take control of Lebanon, where its proxy, Hizbollah [a militant Muslim group and political party based in Lebanon], has ousted a relatively pro-Western prime minister and inserted its own candidate. We've seen the King of Jordan rush to sack his cabinet amid escalating protests. We've seen reports that similar demonstrations are planned for Syria, where the president, Bashar [al-]Assad, will find it far harder to get away with gunning down the crowds than his father did in 1982. And most dramatically, we are seeing the regime in Egypt—the largest, most important Arab country—totter, as President [Hosni] Mubarak faces unprecedented popular protest, and the likelihood that he will have to step down sooner rather than later.

It is tempting to be smug. Egypt's blink-of-an-eye descent into instability underlines afresh the uniqueness of Israel, that embattled sliver of enlightened land in a largely dictatorial region. Those who like to characterise it as the root of all the Middle East's problems look particularly foolish: The people on the streets aren't enraged by Israel, but because their coun-

21

tries are so unlike Israel, so lacking in the freedoms and economic opportunities that both Israeli Jews and Israeli Arabs take for granted.

Yet the country is deeply concerned. The main worry is over a repeat of the events in Iran a little over 30 years ago [in 1979], when popular protest ousted the Shah [a Western-backed authoritarian ruler], only to see him replaced by a far more dangerous, corrupt, misogynist and intolerant regime. Iran is plainly delighted by what is unfolding. With peerless hypocrisy, a government that mowed down its own people less than two years ago [during the Iranian Green Revolution of 2009–2010] is encouraging the same spirit of protest in Egypt. Its allies in the Muslim Brotherhood [an Islamic opposition group in Egypt] are well placed to fill any leadership vacuum—and, for all the group's dubious claims to be relatively moderate, it embraces leadership figures deeply hostile to Israel and to the West. The Muslim Brotherhood, it should not be forgotten, gave birth to Hamas, the terrorist group which now runs Gaza [one of the Palestinian territories], after killing hundreds in its takeover.

The danger for the Egyptians is that, when the protests are over, their brave efforts will have replaced Mubarak not with a leadership more committed to freedom and democracy, but quite the reverse. Yet for Israelis, it underlines the challenges we face when it comes to peacemaking.

*Egypt's blink-of-an-eye descent into instability underlines afresh the uniqueness of Israel, that embattled sliver of enlightened land in a largely dictatorial region.*

## Israel's Danger

Our country, it is often forgotten, is 1/800th of the size of the Arab world, only nine miles wide at its narrowest point. We are not some territorial superpower that can afford not to care if there is hostility all around: We desperately need normalised relations with our neighbours. But if we do a lousy deal, with a regime that is either unstable or not genuinely committed to reconciliation, the consequences could be fatal.

Israelis, I believe, would make almost any territorial compromise in the cause of genuine peace. But where both the Palestinians and the Syrians are concerned, we're far from certain that we have a dependable partner. And as the Egyptian experience is demonstrating, even our most concrete certainties can turn fluid overnight.

For half of Israel's life span, our alliance with Egypt has been central to our foreign policy and military strategy. To achieve it, we relinquished every last inch of the Sinai desert— and, until this weekend, we scarcely had a reason to question that decision. Yes, it's been a cold peace: There's been no profound acceptance of Israel among ordinary Egyptians, or the country's media and professional guilds. Yet Egypt under Mubarak has been less critical of Israel than most other Arab states, gradually intensifying the effort to prevent the smuggling of missiles, rockets and other weaponry into Hamas-controlled Gaza. The absence of war on our Egyptian border has also freed our strained military forces to focus on other, more threatening frontiers.

Over the past two years, as Turkey has moved out of the Western orbit, our other vital regional alliance has slipped away. Now Egypt could also be lost—at a time when Iran and its nuclear ambitions cast an ever greater shadow over the region, and over Israel's future.

---

*For half of Israel's life span, our alliance with Egypt has been central to our foreign policy and military strategy.*

---

But perhaps the most profound concern is over the reversal of momentum that the Egyptian protests could come to represent. For a generation, Israel has been trying to widen

---

## Mubarak Falls

An 18-day-old revolt led by the young people of Egypt ousted President Hosni Mubarak on Friday [February 11, 2011], shattering three decades of political stasis here and overturning the established order of the Arab world.

Shouts of "God is great" erupted from Tahrir Square at twilight as Mr. Mubarak's vice president and longtime intelligence chief, Omar Suleiman, announced that Mr. Mubarak had passed all authority to a council of military leaders.

Tens of thousands who had bowed down for evening prayers leapt to their feet, bouncing and dancing in joy. "Lift your head high, you're an Egyptian," they cried. Revising the tense of the revolution's rallying cry, they chanted, "The people, at last, have brought down the regime."

*David D. Kirkpatrick,*
*"Egypt Erupts in Jubilation as Mubarak Steps Down,"*
New York Times, *February 11, 2011.*

---

the circle of normalisation—to win acceptance as a state among states. We made peace with Egypt, then with Jordan. We built ties with Morocco and the Gulf. We have reached out to the Syrians and Palestinians.

## Momentum Reversing

Now, for the first time in more than 30 years, we see that momentum reversing. We wonder whether Egypt will continue to constitute a stable partner. We worry about the potential for instability in Jordan. We see that all our borders are now "in play"—that the Israel Defense Forces must overhaul their strategy to meet the possibility of dangers in every direction.

We had hoped that the Israeli-Egyptian peace treaty of 1979 would come to be the defining event of the modern era.

Now, we fear that our world will be defined by another event from that year: Iran's dismal Islamic revolution.

# Unrest in Syria Has Divided Opinion in the Israeli-Occupied Golan Heights

*Agence France-Presse*

*Agence France-Presse (AFP) is a French news agency. In the following viewpoint, it reports that people in the Israeli-occupied Golan Heights are split on their attitudes toward protests in Syria. People in the Golan Heights generally consider themselves Syrians, the AFP says. It reports that many in the Golan Heights support Syrian president Bashar al-Assad and believe that the protests against him are a foreign plot. Many others in the Golan Heights, however, would like to see reform in Syria and support the protestors.*

As you read, consider the following questions:

1. According to AFP, why are some in the Golan Heights afraid to express support too publicly for protestors in Syria?
2. How many Syrian nationals are there in the Golan Heights, according to AFP?
3. When does AFP say the Syrian Independence Day celebration was scheduled in the Golan Heights, and what happened to it?

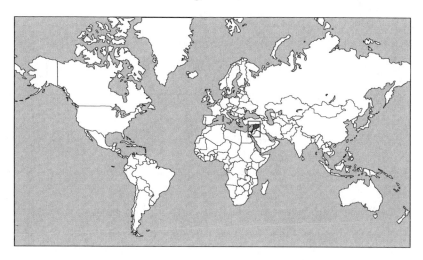

In the Israeli-occupied Golan Heights, people keep a close eye on life back in Syria, which they consider home, and political unrest there has left the local community both anxious and divided.

## A Community Split

In recent weeks [April 2011], the Druze [a monotheistic religion related to Islam] town of Majdal Shams has been watching pro-reform demonstrators staging protests in cities across Syria, demanding more political freedom and an end to repressive emergency laws.

The unrest has split public opinion here, where most residents identify themselves as Syrian and usually stage an annual celebration on Syrian Independence Day.

A few residents openly back the uprising against Syrian President Bashar [al-]Assad's regime, but others say they are afraid to express support too publicly, fearing for the safety of their relatives inside Syria.

And for some in Majdal Shams, the pro-reform protests are nothing more than a foreign plot, stirred up by outsiders in a bid to destabilize Syria.

Earlier this month, around 2,000 people demonstrated in support of Assad's regime in the Golan village of Buq'ata, carrying giant Syrian flags and portraits of the Syrian leader.

---

*For some in Majdal Shams, the pro-reform protests are nothing more than a foreign plot, stirred up by outsiders in a bid to destabilize Syria.*

---

But a smaller group Saturday gathered in Majdal Shams to show solidarity with anti-regime demonstrators across the border.

Around 150 people rallied in the town's main square, some carrying Syrian flags and others holding banners reading "No to killing, no to the regime, no to oppression" and "The people want the liberation of the Golan."

Despite taking part in the demonstration, many protesters had been reluctant to speak to the media, saying their signs and banners said all they would say.

## Against the Dictator

But Shadi Nasrallah told AFP [Agence France-Presse] it was important for the Golan's Druze to participate in the uprising against Assad.

"We are here to support all the people in Syria who are asking for freedom and who oppose the Syrian dictator," he said.

"We are part of Syrian society so we are all against the dictator."

There are about 18,000 Syrian nationals, most of them Druze, in the Golan Heights, which Israel occupied in the 1967 Middle East war and unilaterally annexed in 1981.

Another protester, 25-year-old lawyer and blogger Shefaa Abu Jabal, said the demonstration was intended as a "supportive step by the people of the Golan in solidarity with the revolution of the Syrian people."

---

*"We are part of Syrian society so we are all against the dictator."*

---

Abu Jabal was more cautious about expressing opposition to Assad's regime, saying the protests in the Golan and Syria were mainly seeking reform.

"From the beginning, the revolution has called for reforms and freedom, no one demanded the fall of the regime," he said.

But he acknowledged that the goals of the uprising might not be possible without Assad's removal from office.

"I want freedom for the Syrians, and if the fall of the regime is the price or the way, then I am for it."

As he spoke, a small pro-Assad protest was being staged nearby, which eventually spilled over into a scuffle between some of the younger participants in both demonstrations.

"Most of what is happening in Syria is a conspiracy against Syria, the resistance, the approach of the leadership and President Bashar al-Assad," said Imad Abu Maraei.

But Abu Jamal said there were many people in the Golan who were angered by the often deadly response of Syrian security forces to protests in the country.

"There are people here who are against the regime, but there are also people who are against what is happening there who won't say it," he told AFP.

For people in the Golan, the political unrest across the border has already had a tangible effect.

This year's annual Syrian Independence Day celebration, scheduled for April 17, was cancelled, and anti-regime Druze in the area instead held a general strike in support of protesters across the border.

# Iran, Not Israel, Is the Real Danger in the Middle East

## David M. Weinberg

*David M. Weinberg is the director of public affairs at the Begin-Sadat Center for Strategic Affairs at Bar-Ilan University in Israel. In the following viewpoint, he argues that the unrest in the Middle East has prompted Western observers to argue that Israel is an obstacle to peace. He says that, on the contrary, Israel has little to do with the unrest in the region that is instead directed at toppling dictatorial Arabic regimes. Weinberg argues that the real cause of turmoil is not Israel, but Iran, which he says is attempting to obtain nuclear weapons and is exporting Islamic radicalism throughout the region.*

As you read, consider the following questions:

1. What does Weinberg say are the two insidious arguments that make up the emerging anti-Israeli mythology?
2. According to Weinberg, what fact reinforces Israel's insistence on secure borders?
3. Name a few countries where Weinberg claims Iran seeks to export its form of Islam.

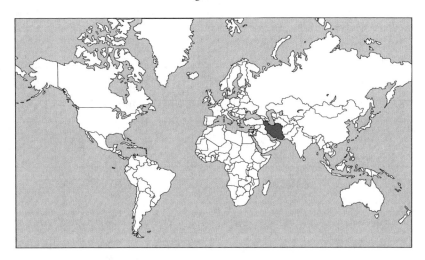

With all the attention being accorded to Arab uprisings of the past month [January–February 2011] in Tunisia, Egypt, Libya, Yemen and Bahrain, the real Middle East menace, Iran, seems all but forgotten. Adding injury to imprudence, a mythology is developing which replaces the Iranian threat with Israel—the new, true threat to regional stability.

## Adding Injury to Imprudence

Two insidious arguments make up this emerging mythology: that Israeli unwillingness to speed towards peace with the Palestinians threatens to further destabilize the Middle East at a sensitive time; and that Israel is on the wrong side of history because it seeks to chill Western enthusiasm for glorious Tahrir Square-style Muslim revolutions. [Tahrir Square was a center of the Egyptian protests in early 2011.]

The first contention is being advanced both by Western leaders and the Israeli Left. We've heard it from German Chancellor Angela Merkel and former US National Security Advisor James Jones: The Israeli-Palestinian conflict is the core dispute that inflames all others. Israel's failure to reach a settlement with [the president of the Palestinian Authority, Mahmoud] Abbas strengthens and amplifies the appeal of the radicals.

Palestine must be created now to contain the Islamist threat and placate Arab public opinion.

The Israeli Left has a twist on this argument: Israel needs to settle rapidly with the Palestinians because we can't hack so many confrontations simultaneously. We need to divert our military and diplomatic resources from the Palestinian arena to the new front lines emerging in Lebanon and Egypt. Settle with Abbas now, so that we can better confront [militant leader Hasan] Nasrallah and the next Ayatollah [religious leader] of Egypt.

Of course, both groups ignore the fact that nobody is demonstrating in Cairo [Egypt] or Sana'a [Yemen] because of Palestine; they ignore the fact that Israel has nobody with whom to negotiate reasonable concessions (Abbas prefers a UN [United Nations] battering ram to negotiations); and they ignore the fact that the Tahrir Square squalls are likely to blow into Ramallah's Manara Square. [Ramallah is a city in the Palestinian West Bank.] The latter fact only reinforces Israel's insistence on secure borders, something that Abbas' shaky, temporary regime is unlikely to be able to provide.

So don't lay the blame on Israel, please, for instability across the Middle East or expect Jerusalem to take wild leaps in order to calm the protestors in Cairo.

## Sinister Contentions

The second sinister contention, advanced by *New York Times* columnist Tom Friedman, among others, is that Israel is a cranky, narrow-minded party pooper because it doesn't feel the joy of freedom being rung-in across the Arab Middle East.

At best, Israel is unnecessarily traumatized by fear and unable to see opportunities beyond the tip of its own nose. At worst, Israeli leaders are "propaganda point seeking" opportunists, says Friedman, who greedily want to keep democracy all for themselves. Those damn Jews, he seems to be saying, always trying to make a buck off the situation for their own

# Will Israel Attack Iran?

It is possible that at some point in the next 12 months [from September 2010], the imposition of devastating economic sanctions on the Islamic Republic of Iran will persuade its leaders to cease their pursuit of nuclear weapons. It is also possible that Iran's reform-minded Green Movement will somehow replace the mullah-led regime, or at least discover the means to temper the regime's ideological extremism. It is possible, as well, that "foiling operations" conducted by the intelligence agencies of Israel, the United States, Great Britain, and other Western powers—programs designed to subvert the Iranian nuclear effort through sabotage and, on occasion, the carefully engineered disappearances of nuclear scientists—will have hindered Iran's progress in some significant way. It is also possible that President [Barack] Obama, who has said on more than a few occasions that he finds the prospect of a nuclear Iran "unacceptable," will order a military strike against the country's main weapons and uranium-enrichment facilities.

But none of these things—least of all the notion that Barack Obama, for whom initiating new wars in the Middle East is not a foreign-policy goal, will soon order the American military into action against Iran—seems, at this moment, terribly likely. What is more likely, then, is that one day next spring, the Israeli national-security adviser, Uzi Arad, and the Israeli defense minister, Ehud Barak, will simultaneously telephone their counterparts at the White House and the Pentagon, to inform them that their prime minister, Benjamin Netanyahu, has just ordered roughly one hundred F-15Es, F-16Is, F-16Cs, and other aircraft of the Israeli air force to fly east toward Iran.

*Jeffrey Goldberg, "The Point of No Return,"*
*Atlantic, September 2010.*

niggardly purposes. Naturally then, unnamed [US President Barack] Obama administration officials—people that Friedman conveniently conjures up—are said to be "thoroughly disgusted" with Israel.

Friedman's remarks, sadly, have the scent of incitement against, and demonization of, Israel.

The charitable interpretation is that Friedman and his fellow travelers are just punch-drunk from partying with the twitterers in Cairo [news of the protests in Egypt were spread through Twitter]. They simplistically encourage the Arab mobs, even though the chances for real democratization anywhere in the Arab world are slim.

---

*At least part of the remedy to these malevolent indictments of Israel is the redirecting of political attentions to the place they most urgently belong: Tehran.*

---

They forget [former US president Jimmy] Carter administration support for the "people's revolution" in Tehran [in 1979]—which gave us the ayatollahs. They forget the much-hailed Lebanese "cedar revolution" of 2005—which gave way within six years to Hizballahstan. [Hizballah is a militant Islamic group; as a political party it has been part of Lebanon's government.] They forget US insistence on Palestinian elections in 2006—which gave us Hamastan in Gaza. [Hamas, a militant Islamic group, won elections in the Palestinian territory of Gaza.] They forget their sanguinity about Turkey's Islamic AKP [the ruling elected political party in Turkey]—which has turned Ankara [Turkey's capital] into an Iranian ally. Friedman's road to hell is paved with good intentions.

Of course, Friedman and friends aren't demanding democracy in the Palestinian Authority. That would threaten Abbas' rule and the Israeli withdrawal they so insist on.

At least part of the remedy to these malevolent indictments of Israel is the redirecting of political attentions to the place they most urgently belong: Tehran.

---

*Iran is the country funding Hizballah and Hamas and weakening Mahmoud Abbas, not Israel. Iran is seeking nuclear weapons with which to dominate the entire region, not Israel.*

---

Iran is the contagion infecting and inflaming the region, not Israel. Iran is the country actively seeking to export its radical blend of Islam to Egypt, Jordan, Lebanon, Yemen, Somalia, Bahrain, Oman, Iraq, Kuwait and Saudi Arabia. Iran is the country seeking to foment instability and to undermine the (somewhat more) pro-Western regimes in the region.

Iran is the country funding Hizballah and Hamas and weakening Mahmoud Abbas, not Israel. Iran is seeking nuclear weapons with which to dominate the entire region, not Israel. Iran is exploiting the festivities in Tahrir Square to advance its ambitious and self-centered agenda, not Israel. Iran is the pernicious opportunist, not Israel.

Israel cannot allow ill-advised Western leaders or ill-willed pundits to propagate new myths that make Israel the fall guy for Western fears of a crumbling Middle East. Back to Iran.

# Iran Is Not a Real Danger

*Yousef Munayyer*

*Yousef Munayyer is a Palestinian-born American writer and political analyst; he is executive director of the Jerusalem Fund. In the following viewpoint, Munayyer argues that the presence of Palestinians living in Israel, as well as the certainty of nuclear retaliation, would prevent Iran from launching a nuclear attack on Israel. He says that Iran is not a real threat, but that Israel needs to create enemies to justify its refusal to resolve its conflict with the Palestinians and withdraw from the Palestinian territories.*

As you read, consider the following questions:

1. How did Benny Morris shock many Israelis and Palestinians, according to Munayyer?
2. What does Munayyer say the ideology at the foundation of the state of Israel requires?
3. According to Munayyer, peace treaties with what countries should have reduced Israel's need for blockades and settlement expansions?

Palestinians are in Israel today because they managed to survive the depopulation of 1948, the year the Jewish state was founded (Arabs constitute about 20% of Israel's population). Ironically, while Benny Morris' scholarship sug-

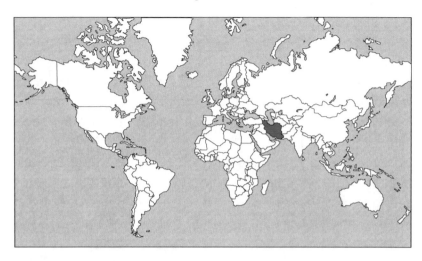

gests that the mere existence of these Palestinians in Israel—and millions more in the occupied territories—irks him, Israel's substantial Arab population also blows a hole in his argument about the need to deal with the supposed Iranian nuclear threat. [Editor's note: Benny Morris is an Israeli historian; this viewpoint is a response to a column by him in the *Los Angeles Times*.]

## Impending Apocalypse

Morris is part of an increasingly vociferous chorus warning of an impending apocalypse for Israel at the hands of a nuclear Iran eager to rid the Middle East of its Jews. Yet Iran's religious leaders have repeatedly stated that such weapons are "un-Islamic" or "forbidden under Islam."

Morris' role in our understanding of the region's history is confounding. Arguably, no one played a more central role in exposing Israel's role in the depopulation of Palestinians from their homeland than Morris. In his seminal work, *The Birth of the Palestinian Refugee Problem*, Morris, using declassified military documents, exposes the calculated effort by early Israeli leaders to impose a Jewish majority through ethnic cleansing.

Long considered a champion of modern Israeli historians who sought to shed light on the ugly side of Israel's birth, Morris shocked many Israelis and Palestinians alike when he later changed course. To Morris, the ethnic cleansing of the Palestinians was no longer the problem at the heart of the conflict; in fact, he suggested that the problem was that Israel didn't finish the job in 1948.

Morris said in a 2004 interview, "Under some circumstances expulsion is not a war crime. I don't think that the expulsions of 1948 were war crimes. You can't make an omelet without breaking eggs. You have to dirty your hands."

---

*The pesky Palestinian minority . . . serves as a deterrent from a nuclear-armed Iran, should the Islamic republic ever build nuclear weapons and consider using them on Israel.*

---

Morris added later in the interview that if Israel's first prime minister, David Ben-Gurion, "was already engaged in expulsion, maybe he should have done a complete job.... If he had carried out a full expulsion—rather than a partial one—he would have stabilized the state of Israel for generations."

Yet the pesky Palestinian minority Morris wishes had been expelled decades ago serves as a deterrent from a nuclear-armed Iran, should the Islamic republic ever build nuclear weapons and consider using them on Israel. The fact that Arab Israelis were among the casualties of the 2006 war with Hezbollah [that is, between Israel and Lebanon, controlled by militant Islamic party Hezbollah] speaks to the reality that no nuclear attack on Israel could happen without the deaths of countless Palestinians and Israelis, not to mention the likely destruction of Jerusalem, the third holiest site in Islam.

The reality of Palestinian casualties, the destruction of Jerusalem, the onset of regional war and the immediate de-

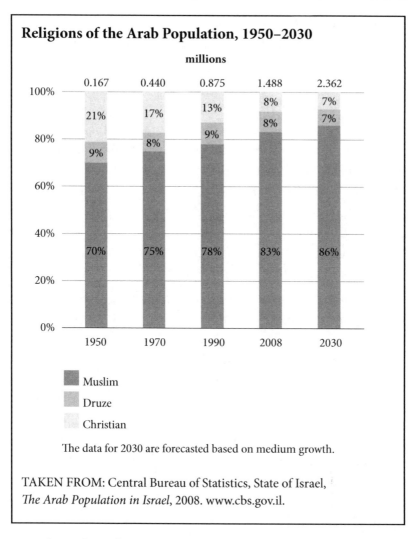

## Religions of the Arab Population, 1950–2030

### millions

The data for 2030 are forecasted based on medium growth.

TAKEN FROM: Central Bureau of Statistics, State of Israel,
*The Arab Population in Israel*, 2008. www.cbs.gov.il.

struction of Iran's regime as a result of a multilateral conventional or even nuclear counterattack all serve as a credible deterrent to a nuclear Iran. The Iranian leadership has shown a demonstrable interest in self-preservation.

## Israel Needs Enemies

The alarmism espoused [by] Morris and company isn't grounded in reality. Rather—just as with Iraq, Syria and now Iran—Israel constantly needs an enemy that it says threatens its existence. Otherwise the Jewish state would have a harder time maintaining its overwhelming military supremacy in the region and continuously changing the subject from resolving the Israeli-Palestinian conflict to practically anything else.

The ideology at the foundation of the state of Israel and the very justification for its existence requires the existence of apocalyptic anti-Semitic forces with the intent and capability to annihilate. Without these boogeymen, whether it is Saddam Hussein [former president of Iraq], Iranian President Mahmoud Ahmadinejad or Arabs who "want to push Israel into the sea," the state of Israel ceases to have any justification for the maintenance of a Jewish majority by force or for its ongoing occupation of Palestinian lands.

The fact that Benjamin Netanyahu, the pro-colonization Israeli prime minister, has made every effort to connect the idea of a nuclear Iran to the Holocaust is evidence of this scaremongering. Iran, like Iraq in 2003, is an inflated but necessary fear for Israel. No credible analysis of the situation envisions a scenario in which Iran would use nuclear weapons against the Jewish state. But proponents of Israel's colonial enterprise, who support maintaining a Jewish majority by the force of walls and soldiers in occupied territory, want everyone to believe that the focus should be on Iran, not on the occupation, and that Israel's security policies are justifiable against "existential threats."

---

*Israel constantly needs an enemy that it says threatens its existence.*

---

The need for these inflated threats has increased in the years since Israel signed peace treaties with Egypt and Jordan. Despite these agreements, Israel still maintains and furthers its occupation of Palestinian lands through blockade and settlement expansion.

The emperor may be naked in Tel Aviv [the capital of Israel], but he can continue avoiding attention and shame if he persuades the world to look in Tehran's [the capital of Iran's] direction instead.

# Israel's Attack on a Syrian Nuclear Power Plant Has Had Mixed Results

*Erich Follath and Holger Stark*

*Erich Follath and Holger Stark are reporters for the German newspaper* Der Spiegel. *In the following viewpoint, they report that in September 2007 Israel launched an attack on and destroyed a Syrian complex devoted to developing nuclear technology. The authors say that both Syrians and Israelis hushed up the incident. The attack was successful in destroying Syria's nuclear capability. However, the attack did little to dissuade Iran from pursuing nuclear weapons, and in that sense, according to the authors, the mission was a failure.*

As you read, consider the following questions:

1. What risky undertaking did Olmert approve in August 2007, according to the authors?

2. What sensational political step do the authors believe Assad was contemplating in 2009 to improve relations with the West?

3. Why do the authors believe that an attack on Iran's nuclear capacity would be much more complex than the Israelis' past attack on plants in Iraq and Syria?

Erich Follath and Holger Stark, "The Story of 'Operation Orchard': How Israel Destroyed Syria's Al Kibar Nuclear Reactor," translated by Christopher Sultan, *Spiegel*, November 2, 2009. www.spiegel.de. Reproduced with permission.

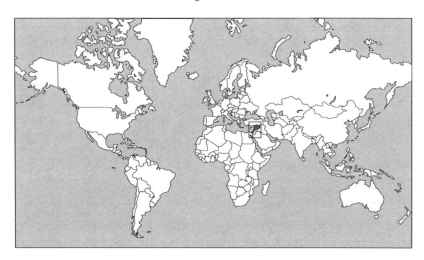

What happened in the night of Sept. 6, 2007 in the desert, 130 kilometers (81 miles) from the Iraqi border, 30 kilometers from Deir el-Zor [in Syria], is one of the great mysteries of our times.

## "This Incident Never Occurred"

At 2:55 p.m. on that day, the Damascus-based Syrian Arab News Agency (SANA) reported that Israeli fighter jets coming from the Mediterranean had violated Syrian airspace at "about one o'clock" in the morning. "Air defense units confronted them and forced them to leave after they dropped some ammunition in deserted areas without causing any human or material damage," a Syrian military spokesman said, according to the news agency. There was no explanation whatsoever for why such a dramatic event was concealed for half a day.

At 6:46 p.m., Israeli government radio quoted a military spokesman as saying: "This incident never occurred." At 8:46 p.m., a spokesperson for the US State Department said during a daily press briefing that he had only heard "second-hand reports" which "contradict" each other.

To this day, Syria and Israel, two countries that have technically been at war since the founding of the Jewish state in

1948, have largely adhered to a bizarre policy of downplaying what was clearly an act of war. Gradually it became clear that the fighter pilots did not drop some random ammunition over empty no-man's land on that night in 2007, but had in fact deliberately targeted and destroyed a secret Syrian complex.

Was it a nuclear plant, in which scientists were on the verge of completing the bomb? Were North Korean, perhaps even Iranian experts, also working in this secret Syrian facility? When and how did the Israelis learn about the project, and why did they take such a great risk to conduct their clandestine operation? Was the destruction of the Al Kibar complex meant as a final warning to the Iranians, a trial run of sorts intended to show them what the Israelis plan to do if Tehran [Iran's capital city] continues with its suspected nuclear weapons program? . . .

---

*Was the destruction of the Al Kibar complex meant as a final warning to the Iranians?*

---

## A New Syrian President

In July 2000, Bashar [al-]Assad succeeded his deceased father, former President Hafez [al-]Assad. The Israelis believed that the younger Assad, a politically inexperienced ophthalmologist who had lived in London for many years and who was only 34 when he took office, would be a weak leader. Unlike his father, an unscrupulous political realist nicknamed "The Lion" who had almost struck a deal with the Israelis over the Golan Heights [a Syrian territory occupied by Israel] in the last few months of his life, Bashar [al-]Assad was considered relatively unpredictable.

According to Israeli agents in Damascus [the Syrian capital], the younger Assad was trying to consolidate his power by espousing radical and controversial positions. He supplied massive amounts of weapons to the Iranian-backed Hezbollah [a Muslim militant group] in Lebanon, for their "struggle for independence" from the "Zionist regime." He received high-ranking delegations from North Korea. The Mossad [Israeli intelligence] was convinced that the subject of these secret talks was a further upgrading of Syria's military capabilities. Pyongyang [the North Korean capital] had already helped Damascus in the past in the development of medium-range ballistic missiles and chemical weapons like sarin and mustard gas. But when Israeli military intelligence informed their Mossad counterparts that a Syrian nuclear program was apparently under discussion, the intelligence professionals were dismissive.

Nuclear weapons for Damascus, a nuclear plant literally on Israel's doorstep? For the experts, it seemed much too implausible. . . .

In late 2006, Israeli military intelligence decided to ask the British for their opinion. But almost at the same time as the delegation from Tel Aviv was arriving in London, a senior Syrian government official checked into a hotel in the exclusive London neighborhood of Kensington. He was under Mossad surveillance and turned out to be incredibly careless, leaving his computer in his hotel room when he went out. Israeli agents took the opportunity to install a so-called "Trojan horse" program, which can be used to secretly steal data, onto the Syrian's laptop.

---

*After being briefed, then [Israeli] Prime Minister Ehud Olmert asked: "Will the reactor be up and running soon, and is there a need to take action?"*

---

The hard drive contained construction plans, letters and hundreds of photos. The photos, which were particularly revealing, showed the Al Kibar complex at various stages in its development. At the beginning—probably in 2002, although the material was undated—the construction site looked like a tree house on stilts, complete with suspicious-looking pipes leading to a pumping station at the Euphrates. Later photos show concrete piers and roofs, which apparently had only one function: to modify the building so that it would look unsuspicious from above. In the end, the whole thing looked as if a shoebox had been placed over something in an attempt to conceal it. But photos from the interior revealed that what was going on at the site was in fact probably work on fissile material. . . .

By now, both Israeli military intelligence and the Mossad were on high alert. After being briefed, then Prime Minister Ehud Olmert asked: "Will the reactor be up and running soon, and is there a need to take action?" Hard to say, the experts said. The prime minister asked for more detailed information, preferably from firsthand. . . .

## A Devastating Report

Olmert was kept apprised of the latest developments. In March 2007, three senior experts from the political, military and intelligence communities were summoned to his residence on Gaza Street in Jerusalem, where Olmert swore them to absolute secrecy. The trio was to advise him on matters relating to the Syrian nuclear program. Olmert wanted results, knowing that he would have to gain the support of the Americans before launching an attack. At the very least, he needed the Americans' tacit consent if he planned to send aircraft into regions that were only a few dozen kilometers from military bases in Turkey, a NATO [North Atlantic Treaty Organization] member.

In August, Major General Yaakov Amidror, the trio's spokesman, delivered a devastating report to the prime minister. While the Mossad had tended to be reserved in its assessment of Al Kibar, the three men were now more than convinced that the site posed an existential threat to Israel and that there was evidence of intense cooperation between Syria and North Korea. There also appeared to be proof of connections to Iran. Mohsen Fakhrizadeh-Mahabadi, who experts believed was the head of Iran's secret "Project 111" for outfitting Iranian missiles with nuclear warheads, had visited Damascus in 2005. Iranian President Mahmoud Ahmadinejad traveled to Syria in 2006, where he is believed to have promised the Syrians more than $1 billion (€675 million) in assistance and urged them to accelerate their efforts.

According to this version of the story, Al Kibar was to be a backup plant for the heavy-water reactor under construction near the Iranian city of Arak, designed to provide plutonium to build a bomb if Iran did not succeed in constructing a weapon using enriched uranium. "Assad apparently thought that, with his weapon, he could have a nuclear option for an Armageddon," says Aharon Ze'evi-Farkash, the former director of Israeli military intelligence.

Olmert approved a highly risky undertaking: a fact-finding mission by Israeli agents on foreign soil. On an overcast night in August 2007, says intelligence expert Ronen Bergman, Israeli elite units traveling in helicopters at low altitude crossed the border into Syria, where they unloaded their testing equipment in the desert near Deir el-Zor and took soil samples in the general vicinity of the Al Kibar plant. The group had to abort its daring mission prematurely when it was discovered by a patrol. The Israelis still lacked the definitive proof they needed. However those in Tel Aviv who favored quick action argued that the results of the samples "provided evidence of the existence of a nuclear program."...

At the time, no one was claiming that Al Kibar represented an immediate threat to Israel's security. Nevertheless, Olmert wanted to attack, despite the tense conditions in the region, the Iraq crisis and the conflict in the Gaza Strip. Olmert notified then US National Security Advisor Stephen Hadley and gave his own military staff the authority to bomb the Syrian plant. The countdown for Operation Orchard had begun.

## The Attack

*Ramat David Air Base, Sept. 5, 2007* Israel's Ramat David air base is located south of the port city of Haifa. It is also near Megiddo, which according to the Bible will be the site of Armageddon, the final battle between good and evil.

The order that the pilots in the squadron received shortly before 11 p.m. on Sept. 5, 2007, seemed purely routine: They were to be prepared for an emergency exercise. All 10 available aircraft, known affectionately by their pilots as "Raam" ("Thunder"), took off into the night sky and headed westward, out into the Mediterranean. It was a maneuver designed to deflect attention from the extraordinary mobilization that had been taking place behind the scenes.

---

*Israel, Olmert said, did not want to play up the incident and was still interested in making peace with Damascus . . . if Assad chose not to draw attention to the Israeli strike, he would do the same.*

---

Three of the 10 F-15s were ordered to return home, while the remaining seven continued flying east-northeast, at low altitude, toward the nearby Syrian border, where they used their precision-guided weapons to eliminate a radar station. Within an additional 18 flight minutes, they had reached the area around Deir el-Zor. By then, the Israeli pilots had the coordinates of the Al Kibar complex programmed into their onboard computers. The attack was filmed from the air, and as is always the case with these strikes, the bombs were far more destructive than necessary. For the Israelis, it made little difference whether a few guards were killed or a larger number of people.

Immediately following the brief report from the military ("target destroyed"), Prime Minister Ehud Olmert called Turkish Prime Minister Recep Tayyip Erdogan, explained the situation, and asked him to inform President Assad in Damascus that Israel would not tolerate another nuclear plant—but that no further hostile action was planned. Israel, Olmert said, did not want to play up the incident and was still interested in making peace with Damascus. He added that if Assad chose not to draw attention to the Israeli strike, he would do the same. . . .

## Consequences

"The facility that was bombed was not a nuclear plant, but rather a conventional military installation," Syrian President Bashar [al-]Assad insisted during a *SPIEGEL* interview at his palace near Damascus in mid-January 2009. "We could have struck back. But should we really allow ourselves to be provoked into a war? Then we would have walked into an Israeli trap." What about the traces of uranium? "Perhaps the Israelis dropped it from the air to make us the target of precisely these suspicions."

Damascus, he said, is not interested in becoming a nuclear power, nor does it believe that Tehran is developing the bomb. "Syria is fundamentally opposed to the proliferation of nuclear weapons. We want a nuclear-free Middle East, Israel included."

Assad, outraged over Israeli belligerence in the Gaza Strip, has suspended secret peace talks with the enemy, which had been brokered by Turkey. But it is also abundantly clear that Assad is eager to remove himself from the list of global political pariahs and enter into dialogue with the United States and Europe.

In the autumn of 2009, relations between Damascus and the West seem to be on the mend, probably as the result of American concessions rather than Israeli bombs. French President Nicolas Sarkozy received Assad at the Élysée Palace and

# Syrian President Bashar al-Assad on Iran's Nuclear Program

Assad: I don't believe that Iran is seeking to develop the bomb. Syria is fundamentally opposed to the proliferation of nuclear weapons. We want a nuclear-free Middle East, Israel included.

*SPIEGEL*: Other Arab heads of state clearly see the threat of an Iranian bomb and are concerned about Iran's growing influence. They fear dominance by the Shiite [a Muslim denomination] country.

Assad: The Americans are stoking these fears with their information policy. Washington is interested in the embargo, with which it hopes to weaken Iran.

*SPIEGEL*: Israeli politicians have developed concrete plans to bomb Iranian nuclear facilities. What would such an attack mean for the Middle East?

Assad: That would be the biggest mistake that anyone could make. The consequences would be catastrophic and would destabilize the region for the long term.

Spiegel Online,
*"Interview with Syrian President Bashar Assad,*
*'Peace Without Syria Is Unthinkable,'"*
*January 19, 2009. www.spiegel.de.*

told him that the normalization of relations would depend on the Syrians meeting a provocatively worded condition: "End nuclear weapons cooperation with Iran." In the first week of October, Syrian Deputy Foreign Minister Faisal Mekdad traveled to Washington to meet with his counterparts there. And Saudi Arabia's King Abdullah, with Washington's explicit blessing, went to Damascus in an attempt to make a shift to the moderate camp more palatable for Assad.

President Barack Obama will probably send a US military attaché to Damascus soon, followed by an ambassador. Syria could be removed from the US's list of state sponsors of terrorism, a list which also includes Iran, Cuba and Sudan. The prospect of billions in aid, as well as transfers of high technology, is being held out to Assad. The Syrian president knows that this is probably his only hope to revive his ailing economy in the long term.

---

*Damascus, [the Syrian president] said, is not interested in becoming a nuclear power, nor does it believe that Tehran is developing the bomb.*

---

Relations between Damascus and Tehran have worsened considerably in recent weeks. Western intelligence agencies report that the Iranian leadership is demanding that Syria return—in full and without compensation—substantial shipments of uranium, which it no longer needs now that its nuclear program has been destroyed.

The latest news from Damascus, the ancient city where Saulus turned into Paulus according to the old scripts: According to information *SPIEGEL* has obtained from sources in Damascus, Assad has been considering taking a sensational political step. He is believed to have suggested to contacts in Pyongyang that he is considering the disclosure of his "national" nuclear program, but without divulging any details of cooperation with his North Korean and Iranian partners. Libyan revolutionary leader Moammar Gadhafi reaped considerable benefits from the international community after a similar "confession" about his country's nuclear program.

The reaction from North Korea was swift and extremely harsh: Pyongyang sent a senior government representative to Damascus to inform Syrian authorities that the North Koreans would terminate all cooperation on chemical weapons if

Assad proceeded with his plan. And this regardless whether he mentioned Pyongyang in this context or not.

Tehran's reaction is believed to have been even more severe. Saeed Jalili, the country's leading nuclear negotiator and a close associate of Iran's supreme religious leader, apparently brought along an urgent message from the Ayatollah Ali Khamenei [the main religious leader in Iran] in which Khamenei called Assad's plan "unacceptable" and threatened that it would spell the end of the two countries' strategic alliance and a sharp decline in relations.

According to intelligence sources, Assad has backed down—for the time being. However he is also looking for ways to do business with his enemies, even Israel's hard-line prime minister, Benjamin Netanyahu. Nevertheless, Assad is loath to give up his contacts to Hezbollah and Tehran completely, and he will demand a very high price for the possible recognition of Israel and for playing the role of mediator with Tehran, namely the return of the entire Golan Heights.

---

*Iran is on the verge of becoming a nuclear power.*

---

## Operation Orchard and Iran

Did Operation Orchard make an impression on the Iranians, and did they understand it the way it was probably intended by the Israelis: as a final warning to Tehran?

The Iranians have—literally—entrenched themselves, and not only since the Israeli attack on Syria. Many of the centrifuges they use for uranium enrichment are now operating in underground tunnels. Not even the bunker-busting super-bombs the Pentagon has requested be made available soon, citing "urgent operational requirements," are capable of fully destroying facilities like the one in Natanz.

The Americans—or the Israelis—would have to conduct air strikes for several weeks and destroy more than a dozen known nuclear facilities to set back the Iranian nuclear program by more than a few weeks. It would be a far more complex undertaking than the Israelis' past attacks on the Osirak reactor in Iraq and Syria's Al Kibar nuclear plant. And even after such a comprehensive operation, which would expose them to counterattacks, they could not be entirely sure of having wiped out all key elements of the Iranian nuclear program. Just in September, Tehran surprised the world with the confession that it had built a previously unreported uranium enrichment plant near Qom.

Operation Orchard achieved only one thing: If the Iranians had planned to build a "spare" nuclear plant in Syria, that is, a backup plutonium factory, their plans were thwarted. But Tehran has time on its side. The Iranians are already believed to have reached breakout capacity—in other words, the ability to begin building a nuclear weapon if they so desire. Iran is on the verge of becoming a nuclear power.

And Syria? There is nothing to suggest that Damascus will or is even able to play with fire once again. A conventional factory has in fact been built over the ruins of the Al Kibar plant. There is no access to the plant—for "security reasons," as residents of Deir el-Zor say tersely—at the roadblock near the great river and the desert village of Tibnah.

# Water Scarcity Could Be Used to Build Cooperation Between Arab States and Israel

*Carnegie Endowment for International Peace*

*In the following viewpoint, the Carnegie Endowment for International Peace presents a panel of expert opinions about how water management can be a source of cooperation among Near East countries such as Turkey, Syria, Lebanon, Jordan, and Iraq, as well as between Israel and Palestine. The panelists agree that water management can encourage socioeconomic development and peace. The panelists include Selim Catafago, president of the Litani River Authority in Lebanon; Fadi Comair, president of the Mediterranean Network of Basin Organizations; Paul Salem, director of the Carnegie Middle East Center in the United States; and Sundeep Waslekar, president of Strategic Foresight Group, a think tank based in India.*

As you read, consider the following questions:

1. According to the panelists, what has been the change in the annual discharge of the Jordan River from 1960 to the present?

2. What is the Israeli daily average water consumption, the Jordanian daily average, and the Palestinian daily average, according to the participants?

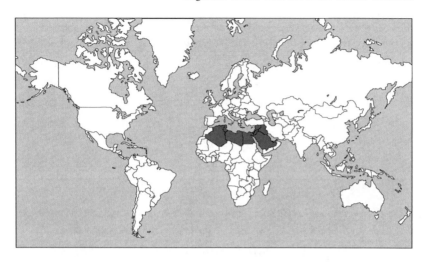

3. What do the panelists say Israelis and Palestinians must agree on before starting to negotiate the terms of water management?

Water resources in the Middle East should be considered as a potential source of socioeconomic development and peace, advocated a recent report ... by the Indian-based think tank Strategic Foresight Group (SFG). At a conference hosted by the Carnegie Middle East Center, in cooperation with SFG, Fadi Comair, president of the Mediterranean Network of Basin Organizations; Selim Catafago, president of the Litani River Authority; and Sundeep Waslekar, president of SFG, discussed the report's main findings and assessed the policy measures that could turn the current regional water crisis into an opportunity to promote development and peace in the Near East. Carnegie's Paul Salem moderated.

While water is often seen as a source of conflict in the Middle East, the panelists noted that water management can be a source of cooperation among Near East countries like Turkey, Syria, Lebanon, Jordan, and Iraq, as well as between Israel and Palestine. As an example of successful cooperation, water management can also create the circumstances necessary for socioeconomic development and peace in these countries.

- Roots of the water crisis: The decrease in water resources—coupled with growing populations that create higher water consumption and the absence of water management—has resulted in a tense political environment. For example, the annual discharge of the Jordan River in 1960 was 1,300 m³ [cubic meters], compared to highs of only about 200 m³ today [2011], even as consumption levels increase at a rapid pace.

- Water to promote peace: Comair argued that if policy makers follow the recommendations made by the Strategic Foresight Group's report and reach a common multinational agreement about the allocation of water resources, this successful cooperation can create what he described as a "peace culture." Such an outcome would "turn this crisis into opportunities for creation," contended Waslekar.

*If policy makers . . . reach a common multinational agreement about the allocation of water resources, this successful cooperation can create . . . a "peace culture."*

To create this peace culture, cooperation in water resource management should be enhanced. The framework for this cooperation is the United Nations convention of 1997, which promotes the use of water in an equitable and reasonable manner in accordance with the needs of individual states. Further guidance for water management cooperation can be derived from European Union directives.

- Hydro-diplomacy: Comair defined hydro-diplomacy as "regional cooperation that creates dynamics of transboundary basin economic development through integrated water resources management." For example, countries along the Jordan River should establish a daily per-capita water usage of under 200 liters, he said. In comparison, today Israelis consume a daily average of 350 liters per capita, while Jordanians consume about 60 liters and Palestinians only about 30 liters.

- Implementing hydro-diplomacy: The report recommends that Near East countries improve water management through the following steps:
  1. Develop the region economically.
  2. Ensure the fulfillment of domestic and water needs in order to improve food security in the region.
  3. Enhance the struggle against climate change and global warming, which reduce river flows and rainfalls and generate droughts and desertification.
  4. Contribute to political stability through equitable sharing of water resources.

## Key Policy Recommendations

Hydro-diplomacy aims to establish two main regional frameworks for water management, which should be actively supported by the international community:

- Establish a cooperation council for water resources: This council should include Turkey, Syria, Iraq, Lebanon, and Jordan, noted Comair. It will serve as a political mechanism to establish common standards for measuring water flow and quality, set goals for sustainable management of water resources, adapt regional strategies to combat climate change and drought, and facilitate basin-level cooperation in each river basin. The organization will also improve the sharing of knowledge and information about water resources among the various countries.

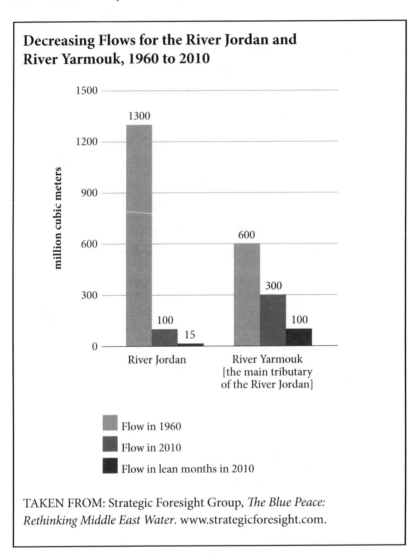

**Decreasing Flows for the River Jordan and River Yarmouk, 1960 to 2010**

TAKEN FROM: Strategic Foresight Group, *The Blue Peace: Rethinking Middle East Water*. www.strategicforesight.com.

- Develop a high-level confidence-building initiative between Israel and the Palestinian Territories: This initiative's key responsibility is to answer the specific challenges caused by the ongoing conflict between Israelis and Palestinians. The current negotiations about water management depend on figures from the Oslo Accords in the early 1990s, even though studies show that water resources have depleted by 7 percent since then. The panelists highlighted the need for the parties to meet and agree on facts and data, even before starting to negotiate the terms of water management. In particular, Catafago explained that the lack of confidence between Israelis and Palestinians is the most important impediment to improving water resource management.

- Encourage the international community to become actively involved: The international community should play a critical support role in both the technical and financial aspects of hydro-diplomacy. The panelists emphasized, however, that the cooperation initiative should emerge from the Near East countries, as it is first and foremost their responsibility.

---

*The lack of confidence between Israelis and Palestinians is the most important impediment to improving water resource management.*

---

A few initiatives have been launched in the past decade, but they all lack a necessary comprehensive approach. For example, Syria and Lebanon signed an agreement in 2002 to exchange information and monitor the flow and quality of the water for the Orontes and the Nahr el-Kebir rivers. However, the construction of a diversion dam on the Orontes was interrupted by Israeli bombings in 2006, showing the crucial need for cooperation and dialogue among all countries.

# Arabs Have Been Weakened by Their Lack of Knowledge of Israel

*Taylor Luck*

*Taylor Luck is an American journalist based in Jordan, where he reports for the English-language paper the* Jordan Times. *In the following viewpoint, he discusses a book by Jordanian political analyst Hassan Barari called* Israelism: Arab Scholarship on Israel, a Critical Assessment. *Barari argues that Arabs and Palestinians have traditionally and simplistically cast Israel as an enemy, without bothering to study and understand the nation. Barari believes that this has put Arabs at a disadvantage in dealing with Israel.*

As you read, consider the following questions:

1. From what book did Barari borrow the title of his own book?

2. Why have Arab researchers and journalists been reluctant to learn Hebrew, according to this viewpoint?

3. According to Barari, why did Jordanian researchers start to produce more analytical studies of Israel in the mid-1990s?

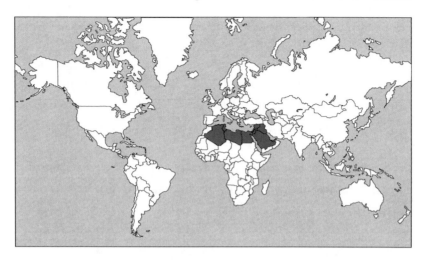

A lack of objective Arab research on Israel has had a profound impact on the Palestinian-Israeli conflict and the history of the entire region over the past half century, according to a recently released book.

## Israelism

In his new book, *Israelism[: Arab Scholarship on Israel, a Critical Assessment]*, Jordanian political analyst, researcher and columnist Hassan Barari borrows his title from Edward Said's seminal work *Orientalism*.

Barari, who read Said's work in a translation class in high school, sees parallels between the two phenomena.

"We have been so critical of Orientalism, how Western scholars don't live here and don't know the language. If I apply the same logic to the way Arabs have written on Israel, we have a similar trend in Israelism," he said, noting that as Said's *Orientalism* concludes that as the Orient was studied by the West in order to be "dominated", Israel is studied in the region with the main aim of singling it out as an enemy.

Barari said there was very little Arab academic writing on Israel in the first three decades of its existence, compared to the wealth of studies on Arab countries, although "biased", written at the same time in Israel.

The resulting lack of objective research resulted in a knowledge deficit that undermined Arab efforts to regain territories and secure Palestinians their land and basic rights, he said.

"We failed miserably at a time when knowledge was power".

Arabs believed at first that Israel was an "artificial entity" and a "passing phenomenon" which would not require any further study, while all efforts to make Israel seem "weak" often led to underestimation of its military and political capabilities.

"We thought that Israeli society would collapse at the first bullet. And it did not, time and time again," he said.

---

*Israel is studied in the region with the main aim of singling it out as an enemy.*

---

A language barrier has also hindered research. As most researchers and journalists tended to be against normalisation with Israel at all levels, they refused to learn Hebrew or converse with Israelis, dramatically impairing Arabs' understanding of Israeli decision making.

Another factor inhibiting Arab research was what he terms as an "inevitability mind-set" which led scholars to believe that as the country was "not likely to last", there was no need to understand domestic happenings in Israel.

## Knowledge Is Power

Between 1948 and the 1970s, Arab nationalists, who dominated the discourse on Israel, viewed Israel as a tool of imperialists looking to take Arab resources and occupy lands, and believed that the study of the West and Russia, but not Israeli domestic politics, was sufficient to understand Israeli actions.

Following the 1967 war, the Islamist movement, particularly the Muslim Brotherhood [an Islamic political opposition group operating in many Arab countries], began to take up the Israeli issue as their own, shaping Israeli studies in the region, according to Barari.

"By the 1980s, Israel proved to have a strong and dynamic society with a GDP [gross domestic product] which was larger than Jordan, Syria, Egypt and Lebanon combined. Views of it collapsing began to wane," he noted.

---

*Between 1948 and the 1970s, Arab nationalists ... viewed Israel as a tool of imperialists looking to take Arab resources and occupy lands.*

---

In the 1980s, the Islamists used the Palestinian-Israeli issue for their own end, believing that only after "Islamising" and "purifying" Arab society could Israel be defeated, an approach that has also discouraged objective study, according to Barari's book, which he researched in Hebrew, Arabic and English with the aid of the United States Institute of Peace.

Only in the mid-1990s, with the Oslo Accords and other peace efforts, did Jordanian scholars begin producing analytical research on Israeli society and politics, he said, noting that further study is still needed in the field.

"We do have good scholars who work on Israel in an objective way, but up until now, the dominant style of writing on the subject has been Israelism," he said, noting that Arab media failed to play "an encouraging role" in accurately depicting developments in Israel, hurting the Arab cause.

*Al Ghad* [newspaper] columnist Jamil Nimri agreed, noting that it was easier for Jordanian journalists to report on Israel during the "good times" between 1994 and 1997, following the 1994 Wadi Araba peace treaty and before the second Intifada [a Palestinian uprising that began in 2000].

"At the time we saw a breakthrough in reporting. There was more interest to see Israelis in a more objective way, because in the end they are also human beings—we could see them in a different kind of light," he said.

Barari, who held a book signing last month [July 2009], expressed hope for greater understanding, which he stressed does not contradict the Arab or Palestinian cause.

"Knowledge is power," he said.

# Periodical and Internet Sources Bibliography

*The following articles have been selected to supplement the diverse views presented in this chapter.*

| | |
|---|---|
| Amnesty International | "Israel Rations Palestinians to Trickle of Water," October 27, 2009. www.amnesty.org. |
| Aluf Benn | "Without Egypt, Israel Will Be Left with No Friends in the Mideast," *Haaretz*, January 29, 2011. |
| Richard Boudreaux and Joshua Mitnick | "Israel Braces for a New Egypt," *Wall Street Journal*, February 10, 2011. |
| Juan Cole | "Wikileaks: Israel Plans Total War on Lebanon, Gaza," *Informed Comment* (blog), January 2, 2011. www.juancole.com. |
| Jeffrey Goldberg | "The Point of No Return," *Atlantic*, September 2010. |
| Glenn Greenwald | "How Propagandists Function: Exhibit A," *Salon*, August 12, 2010. www.salon.com. |
| Yaakov Katz | "Israel Concerned About Hamas-Egypt Relations," *Jerusalem Post*, April 11, 2011. |
| Yossi Melman | "Israel Has Already Attacked Iran," *Haaretz*, January 17, 2011. |
| David E. Miller | "Palestinian Influx into Jordan Is a Fiction," *Jerusalem Post*, March 16, 2011. |
| Anshel Pfeffer | "IDF: Syria May Provoke Israel to Distract from Domestic Unrest," *Haaretz*, March 23, 2011. |
| Edmund Sanders | "All's Quiet on the Israel-Lebanon Front," *Los Angeles Times*, March 6, 2011. |

**GLOBAL**VIEWPOINTS

## CHAPTER 2

# Israel and the Gaza Strip

# Hamas Is a Dangerous Terrorist Organization That Must Be Isolated

*Martin Bright*

*Martin Bright is a British journalist and political editor for the New Statesman. In the following viewpoint, Bright reports that the militant group Hamas damages the Palestinian cause and endangers the people of the Gaza Strip. He believes that the Arab world is paralyzed by internal conflict and that the Hamas government has been reckless with citizens' lives. Bright believes that what Hamas has done and what has occurred in the Gaza Strip cannot be justified.*

As you read, consider the following questions:

1. According to Bright, how has the Hamas government in Gaza treated the lives of its citizens?
2. As stated in the viewpoint, to what does Bright believe the Hamas government is "akin"?
3. Does the author believe Hamas should be defeated?

As the the dust and white phosphorus settle over Gaza, two questions present themselves immediately. What happens if the rockets fired on southern Israel stop? And what if they continue?

If they stop, Israel will feel fully justified in its strategy of a combined air and ground assault on Gaza, which left an estimated 1,300 dead, many of them women and children. If they continue, as appears to be Hamas's suicidal intention, the Israeli army and air force have already shown what the consequences are likely to be.

---

*It is also true that the Hamas government in Gaza has been utterly reckless with the lives of its citizens.*

---

International opinion is largely irrelevant here. The Arab world remains paralysed by its internal divisions, while Western leaders have expressed their horror at the brutality of the war. Amnesty International has called for an investigation into alleged Israeli war crimes in Gaza and this may yet happen. But it will make no difference to the Israeli government's position. When I travelled to Israel earlier this year [2009], there was a clear consensus among the government advisers, soldiers and political analysts I met that Israel was doing the West's dirty work for it by containing Hamas. It is certainly the case that its citizens have been in the front line in Sderot and other southern cities.

It is also true that the Hamas government in Gaza has been utterly reckless with the lives of its citizens. From the outside, the grotesque tally of the dead (over 1,000 versus 13 Israelis) looks hideously unjust. But from inside Israel and Palestine, there is another way of looking at it (and this is bleak, indeed): Which side did best in protecting its own people?

Israel will now argue that the neutralisation of Hamas makes the prospects for a genuine peace based on a two-state solution more likely. Perhaps that's true. It really is impossible to know at this stage.

## What Is Hamas?

Hamas is the largest and most influential Palestinian militant movement. In January 2006, the group won the Palestinian Authority's (PA) general legislative elections, defeating Fatah, the party of the PA's president, Mahmoud Abbas, and setting the stage for a power struggle. Since attaining power, Hamas has continued its refusal to recognize the state of Israel, leading to crippling economic sanctions. Historically, Hamas has sponsored an extensive social service network. The group has also operated a terrorist wing, carrying out suicide bombings and attacks using mortars and short-range rockets.

*Council on Foreign Relations,*
*"Backgrounder: Hamas," August 27, 2009.*
*www.cfr.org.*

## War Crimes in Gaza

But even if you accept, as I do, that Hamas represents a strain of totalitarian Islamist thought akin to fascism, what happened in Gaza cannot be justified. Even if you accept, as I do, that Hamas must be defeated as a military force, this was not the way to go about it. Even if you accept, as I do, that Hamas used women and children as human shields, this does not mean that the terrorist organisation should take the entire blame when Israeli weapons kill innocents.

When I wrote a piece for this magazine last May called "The great betrayal", intended as a critique of the British left's attitude to Israel, it turned out to be one of the most controversial articles I had written. It argued that some opposition to the Zionist state on the left was only explicable as anti-Semitism. I described the Israel-Palestine conflict as "a terrible faultline on the British left". The piece was seen in some quarters as over-sympathetic to Israel, but it contained the following important paragraph: "On the face of it, the answer to my question [Why does the left hate Israel?] is simple. The British left hates Israel because it has abandoned its Enlightenment principles and set about the systematic oppression of a people whose land it occupies. The invasion of southern Lebanon in the summer of 2006 was a new low point that caused international outrage. For most people on the left in Britain, support for Israel is out of the question." Now there is a new low point. However, before we assume that everyone agrees with the left consensus that Israel is to blame, it's worth looking at the recent *Sunday Times*/YouGov poll, which showed that 39 per cent blamed both sides equally and 24 per cent blamed Hamas. Only 18 per cent blamed Israel.

---

*The uncomfortable fact is that many of these groups do have a unifying ideology, which is anti-Enlightenment, anti-women, anti-gay and anti-Semitic.*

---

No one denies that what happened in Gaza is horrible, not even the Israeli government. I was struck by an interview during the conflict, on Radio 4's *Today* programme, with Mark Regev, the Israeli prime minister's tough-talking foreign press spokesman. Asked whether he had any doubts when he saw the results of Israeli bombing, he answered: "Yes, of course I do." Over the past few weeks, Britain's most passionate supporters of Israel have been forced to search deep into their consciences.

On 6 January, when Israel hit a UN [United Nations] school in Gaza, the Britain Israel Communications and Research Centre (Bicom) issued the following statement: "Israeli voices are indicating that there was a hidden weapon store in the school, but clearly there can be no defence of civilian casualties."

# Gaza Dangers

In Britain, the main consequence of the Gaza War has been to provide a rallying point for the motley alliance of totalitarian sympathisers of the hard left and Islamic radical right. It is not the responsibility of the Israeli government to consider the consequences of their actions on the rise of militant Islam in Britain and Europe. But the dangers are real. The Islamist tendency represented by self-appointed representatives such as the Muslim Council of Britain and the Muslim Association of Britain was on the retreat. The Gaza War has given them new life, as shown by their prominence in the recent demonstrations, and across the media.

It is telling that Ed Husain, author of *The Islamist* and one of the most effective opponents of Hamas sympathisers in Britain, issued a statement calling on the British government to intervene with Israel. "The UK government cannot seek to win hearts and minds across Muslim communities while failing to stop Israel from murdering Palestinians en masse," he wrote. More worrying, in a way, is the renewal of an official narrative of compromise with Islamism, as demonstrated by David Miliband's peculiar intervention during his trip to Mumbai where he warned: "The more we lump terrorist groups together and draw the battle lines as a simple binary struggle between moderates and extremists or good and evil, the more we play into the hands of those seeking to unify groups with little in common, and the more we magnify the sense of threat." The uncomfortable fact is that many of these groups do have a unifying ideology, which is anti-Enlightenment, anti-women, anti-gay and anti-Semitic.

I have written widely about the Islamic radical right in Britain and I have always been depressed at the size of the psychological space occupied by the Palestinian struggle in the minds of young British Muslims. It has always seemed peculiar that bright and politically committed members of the Pakistani and Bangladeshi community are so particularly concerned with the alleged abuses of the Israeli government. If half the energy expended by the south Asian diaspora in defence of the Palestinians was spent campaigning for justice and political transparency in Pakistan and Bangladesh, then the prospects for reform in those countries would be vastly enhanced.

To return to my original questions: What happens if the Hamas rockets stop? And what happens if they don't? The awful truth is that either outcome will be used to justify the unjustifiable, whether that is the killing of Israeli innocents by Hamas terrorists in the name of resistance, or the bombing of Palestinian innocents by the Israeli military in the name of national security.

# Israel Should Negotiate with Hamas

### *Johann Hari*

*Johann Hari is a British journalist who writes for the* Independent, Huffington Post, Slate, *and other venues. In the following viewpoint, he argues that tension between the Palestinian factions Fatah and Hamas is caused by Israeli and international pressure on the Palestinian territories. He argues that there is actually substantial support in Gaza for peace. He points out also that Hamas, once elected, behaved in a pragmatic manner. He concludes that Israel must negotiate with Hamas in order to create a chance for peace.*

As you read, consider the following questions:

1. Who is Amal Hellis, according to Hari?
2. What does Hari say Hamas received for its pragmatic approach to government from Israel and the United States?
3. Why does Uri Avnery say that Israel may be thwarting possible peace partners?

The enemies of the Palestinian people have been presenting the political chaos of the past week [June 2007, the conflict involved fighting between Palestinian factions Fatah and

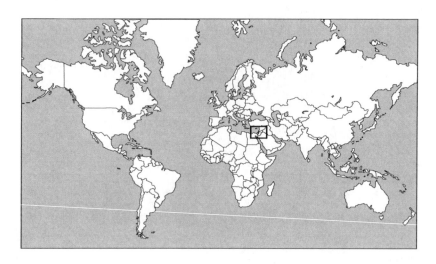

Hamas] as evidence that they are pre-modern savages, capable only of building a Mogadishu [a city in Somalia, a country known for violence and chaos] on the Mediterranean. But on Wednesday afternoon, the real voice of the Palestinian people echoed out, for a fleeting moment.

Thousands of protesters—mostly women—took to the streets. They called not for sharia law or Qassam rockets [simple rockets developed by Hamas] against Israeli cities, but for peace. Amal Hellis, a 35-year-old mother of two, said: "I am not afraid. I will die to save my family and to save Palestine." Her eldest son Medhat is a member of Fatah; her youngest son Refaat belongs to Hamas. When the marchers reached the Al Ghifary tower near the beachfront, they were fired on by gunmen—but they did not run away. The old women and their granddaughters stood in the crossfire, waving Palestinian flags and singing "Give Peace a Chance".

## A Pro-Peace Constituency

Hamas gunmen fired from above; Fatah fighters threatened them on the ground. The women surrounded the Fatah man, forcing him with nothing but plain moral pressure to lower his rifle. Only when one of the protesters was caught in the chest by a sniper did they finally disperse.

These protesters speak for a majority of Palestinians. In the most recent poll of them conducted by the Palestinian Center for Policy and Survey Research, 63 per cent supported full recognition of Israel in return for a proper Palestinian state. These supporters of a negotiated peace include, crucially, a majority of Hamas supporters.

---

*The current crackle of civil war is not evidence that the Palestinians are incapable of self-government. It is evidence of what happens to human beings when they are rammed into a pressure cooker.*

---

This means there is actually a bigger pro-peace constituency in Palestine than in Israel, where Hebrew newspaper *Yediot Aharanot* polling just found that 58 per cent of Israelis now reject the idea of trading land for peace, because they think the Palestinians are irrevocably committed to destroying them.

The current crackle of civil war is not evidence that the Palestinians are incapable of self-government. It is evidence of what happens to human beings when they are rammed into a pressure cooker and the temperature is slowly ramped up.

When I was last in Gaza a few months ago, the borders of Palestine had been hermetically sealed by the world for months as punishment for choosing Hamas in a free election. One-and-a-half million people were locked into a tiny space no bigger than the Isle of Wight. Nothing went in; nothing went out. The hospitals were on the brink of collapse because if a piece of equipment broke they could not get new parts. Almost everyone was out of work because they couldn't sell to the world a few miles away.

In this situation, any people, anywhere, would begin to turn on each other. As the Palestinian foreign minister Ziad

## Two Political Systems

The international community, and particularly Israel, seems to hope that punishing economic sanctions and diplomatic isolation will simply make Hamas disappear and render Gaza more pliable or even irrelevant. The Palestinian division, however, prevents the Palestinians from speaking with one voice, much less acting in a coherent manner. This rift would vitiate any diplomatic breakthrough that might occur between Israel and the Palestinians in resolving, or even managing, the conflict.

When Hamas and Fatah fought their brief but bitter civil war in June 2007, the outcome was short of Solomonic: the object of contention, the Palestinian Authority (PA), was actually split in two. The grim reality is that the Palestinians now have two political systems that are moving further away from each other, and neither seems to have a viable strategy for realizing its vision or building a better future for the people it purports to lead.

*Nathan J. Brown,*
*"The Hamas-Fatah Conflict: Shallow but Wide,"*
The Fletcher Forum of World Affairs, *vol. 34, no. 2, 2010.*
*http://fletcher.tuffs.edu.*

Abu Amr puts it: "If you have two brothers put into a cage and deprive them of the basic essential needs for life, they will fight."

On top of this, the outside world has actually discouraged and humiliated the Palestinian moderates. When he took charge in 2005, the Fatah President Mahmoud Abbas made it plain he would offer huge compromises to Israel in return for a state. [Israeli Prime Minister] Ariel Sharon offered him a few lifted roadblocks in return. The message to the Palestinians was clear: electing pragmatists will get you nothing. So the next year, in desperation they elected Hamas, an Islamic fundamentalist organisation whose constitution includes statements from the anti-Semitic forgery, the Protocols of the Elders of Zion.

---

*Regular readers will know that I loathe Hamas, but I have to acknowledge that, upon election, their leaders undeniably behaved in a pragmatic way.*

---

## Behaving Pragmatically

Regular readers will know that I loathe Hamas, but I have to acknowledge that, upon election, their leaders undeniably behaved in a pragmatic way. They did not start introducing the savagery of sharia [Islamic] law, or oppressing women. Instead, they observed the unilateral truce with Israel. They offered a hudna (cease-fire) that would last a generation. They gave up staging suicide-murders against Israeli civilians. They even said they would respect all previous agreements signed by the Palestinian Authority—a de facto concession that they would recognise Israel.

And in return? They received nothing but abuse and a determined attempt to dislodge them from power, by boycott and, more slowly, by bullet. The US and Israel began arming an especially authoritarian wing of Fatah, headed by Mohammed Dahlan, with the plain intention of him toppling Hamas sooner or later. The Washington [D.C.]-based architect of this policy is Deputy National Security Advisor Elliott Abrams, a man who in the 1980s secretly armed the openly fascist Contra militias in an attempt to topple the Sandinista government in Nicaragua. By denying Hamas power through a legitimate election, and arming their enemies for a future liquidation, the US and Israel virtually guaranteed Hamas would seize power.

Why is the Israeli government doing this? There are a range of possible explanations. One, associated with former Prime Minister Bibi [Benjamin] Netanyahu and current Deputy Prime Minister Avigdor Lieberman, is the belief that the Palestinians will only compromise once they have been totally defeated by overwhelming force. They reckon that if the Palestinians are throttled for long enough, sooner or later they will cower, beg for mercy, and accept Israeli terms.

---

*There is still a way out of this. Israel must negotiate with Hamas.*

---

## Expansion over Peace

The next, and more disturbing, explanation is that the Israeli government may be deliberately thwarting potential peace partners. Uri Avnery, a former member of the Israeli Knesset and disillusioned Irgun fighter, explains why: "There has always been a tendency in Israel to prefer expansion and settlement to compromise and peace. Our government has worked for years to destroy Fatah, in order to avoid the need to negotiate an agreement that would inevitably lead to the withdrawal of the settlements from Palestinian land. Now, when it seems this aim has been achieved, they have no idea what to do about the Hamas victory."

There is still a way out of this. Israel must negotiate with Hamas. They are offering a long, long cease-fire. The Arab states are even—in a startling offer from Saudi Arabia—offering full recognition and normalisation of Israel in the region, if only Israel returns to its legal borders. Perhaps they are lying. Perhaps it is a trick. But it is the only game plan in town that offers even the chance of a happy ending.

But Israel seems determined not to take this chance. Ehud Barak, the ex-PM [prime minister] back as Defence Minister, is briefing that he will bomb Gaza yet again, and within weeks.

He is proposing to actually intensify the blockade of the Gaza Strip for a few weeks, to "pressure" Hamas.

The Israeli government is clinging to the belief that the harder you beat the Palestinians, the softer their leaders will become. This mentality created the current collapse. It will only drag the Middle East further and further away from the sane voices of women such as Amal Hellis, singing songs of peace.

# Israel's Actions in the Gaza War Were Justifiable

**Richard Goldstone**

*Richard Goldstone was a justice of the Constitutional Court of South Africa and chaired the United Nations fact-finding mission on the Gaza War of 2008–2009. His report, known as the Goldstone Report, suggested that Israel had committed war crimes. In the following viewpoint, he largely retracts that accusation. Goldstone says that Israel withheld information during his initial fact-finding mission. With the new information, he says, it is clear that Israel did not deliberately target civilians. Hamas, on the other hand, he says, did target civilians and should face strong international censure.*

As you read, consider the following questions:

1. What was the most serious attack the Goldstone Report focused on, according to Goldstone?

2. What does Goldstone say were the main recommendations of the Goldstone Report?

3. According to Goldstone, what lessons were learned and what policies were changed because of the Goldstone Report?

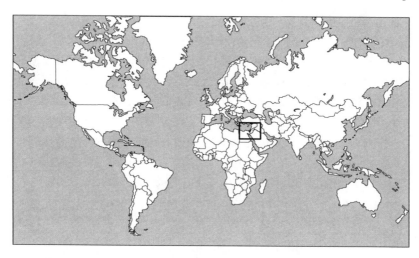

We know a lot more today about what happened in the Gaza war of 2008–09 than we did when I chaired the fact-finding mission appointed by the U.N. Human Rights Council that produced what has come to be known as the Goldstone Report. If I had known then what I know now, the Goldstone Report would have been a different document.

The final report by the U.N. committee of independent experts—chaired by former New York judge Mary McGowan Davis—that followed up on the recommendations of the Goldstone Report has found that "Israel has dedicated significant resources to investigate over 400 allegations of operational misconduct in Gaza" while "the de facto authorities (i.e., Hamas) have not conducted any investigations into the launching of rocket and mortar attacks against Israel."

Our report found evidence of potential war crimes and "possibly crimes against humanity" by both Israel and Hamas. That the crimes allegedly committed by Hamas were intentional goes without saying—its rockets were purposefully and indiscriminately aimed at civilian targets.

The allegations of intentionality by Israel were based on the deaths of and injuries to civilians in situations where our fact-finding mission had no evidence on which to draw any other reasonable conclusion. While the investigations published by the Israeli military and recognized in the U.N. committee's report have established the validity of some incidents that we investigated in cases involving individual soldiers, they also indicate that civilians were not intentionally targeted as a matter of policy.

For example, the most serious attack the Goldstone Report focused on was the killing of some 29 members of the al-Simouni family in their home. The shelling of the home was apparently the consequence of an Israeli commander's erroneous interpretation of a drone image, and an Israeli officer is under investigation for having ordered the attack. While the length of this investigation is frustrating, it appears that an appropriate process is under way, and I am confident that if the officer is found to have been negligent, Israel will respond accordingly. The purpose of these investigations, as I have always said, is to ensure accountability for improper actions, not to second-guess, with the benefit of hindsight, commanders making difficult battlefield decisions.

---

*Civilians were not intentionally targeted as a matter of policy.*

---

While I welcome Israel's investigations into allegations, I share the concerns reflected in the McGowan Davis report that few of Israel's inquiries have been concluded and believe that the proceedings should have been held in a public forum. Although the Israeli evidence that has emerged since publication of our report doesn't negate the tragic loss of civilian life, I regret that our fact-finding mission did not have such evidence explaining the circumstances in which we said civilians in Gaza were targeted, because it probably would have influenced our findings about intentionality and war crimes.

Israel's lack of cooperation with our investigation meant that we were not able to corroborate how many Gazans killed were civilians and how many were combatants. The Israeli military's numbers have turned out to be similar to those recently furnished by Hamas (although Hamas may have reason to inflate the number of its combatants).

As I indicated from the very beginning, I would have welcomed Israel's cooperation. The purpose of the Goldstone Report was never to prove a foregone conclusion against Israel. I insisted on changing the original mandate adopted by the Human Rights Council, which was skewed against Israel. I have always been clear that Israel, like any other sovereign nation, has the right and obligation to defend itself and its citizens against attacks from abroad and within. Something that has not been recognized often enough is the fact that our report marked the first time illegal acts of terrorism from Hamas were being investigated and condemned by the United Nations. I had hoped that our inquiry into all aspects of the Gaza conflict would begin a new era of evenhandedness at the U.N. Human Rights Council, whose history of bias against Israel cannot be doubted.

Some have charged that the process we followed did not live up to judicial standards. To be clear: Our mission was in no way a judicial or even quasi-judicial proceeding. We did not investigate criminal conduct on the part of any individual in Israel, Gaza or the West Bank. We made our recommendations based on the record before us, which unfortunately did not include any evidence provided by the Israeli government. Indeed, our main recommendation was for each party to investigate, transparently and in good faith, the incidents referred to in our report. McGowan Davis has found that Israel has done this to a significant degree; Hamas has done nothing.

Some have suggested that it was absurd to expect Hamas, an organization that has a policy to destroy the state of Israel, to investigate what we said were serious war crimes. It was my hope, even if unrealistic, that Hamas would do so, especially if

Israel conducted its own investigations. At minimum I hoped that in the face of a clear finding that its members were committing serious war crimes, Hamas would curtail its attacks. Sadly, that has not been the case. Hundreds more rockets and mortar rounds have been directed at civilian targets in southern Israel. That comparatively few Israelis have been killed by the unlawful rocket and mortar attacks from Gaza in no way minimizes the criminality. The U.N. Human Rights Council should condemn these heinous acts in the strongest terms.

In the end, asking Hamas to investigate may have been a mistaken enterprise. So, too, the Human Rights Council should condemn the inexcusable and cold-blooded recent slaughter of a young Israeli couple and three of their small children in their beds.

---

*I had hoped that our inquiry into all aspects of the Gaza conflict would begin a new era of evenhandedness at the U.N. Human Rights Council, whose history of bias against Israel cannot be doubted.*

---

I continue to believe in the cause of establishing and applying international law to protracted and deadly conflicts. Our report has led to numerous "lessons learned" and policy changes, including the adoption of new Israel Defense Forces procedures for protecting civilians in cases of urban warfare and limiting the use of white phosphorus in civilian areas. The Palestinian Authority established an independent inquiry into our allegations of human rights abuses—assassinations, torture and illegal detentions—perpetrated by Fatah in the West Bank, especially against members of Hamas. Most of those allegations were confirmed by this inquiry. Regrettably, there has been no effort by Hamas in Gaza to investigate the allegations of its war crimes and possible crimes against humanity.

Simply put, the laws of armed conflict apply no less to non-state actors such as Hamas than they do to national armies. Ensuring that non-state actors respect these principles, and are investigated when they fail to do so, is one of the most significant challenges facing the law of armed conflict. Only if all parties to armed conflicts are held to these standards will we be able to protect civilians who, through no choice of their own, are caught up in war.

# Israel's Actions in the Gaza War Were Indefensible

*Daud Abdullah*

*Daud Abdullah, born in St. David's, Grenada, is the deputy sec-retary general of the Muslim Council of Britain. In the following viewpoint, he argues that Israel launched a war on Gaza and has occupied and persecuted the Palestinian people for decades. He says that the West, particularly the United States and Brit-ain, have protected Israel from having to answer to international law for its actions. He concludes that Israel should be held ac-countable for war crimes.*

As you read, consider the following questions:

1. What international actions have been taken against war criminals in the Congo, Sri Lanka, and Sudan, according to Abdullah?
2. What does Abdullah say that the United States did in 2004 to protect Israel from the International Court of Justice?
3. According to Abdullah, how much of historic Palestine does Israel occupy?

Following Richard Goldstone's rather odd op-ed piece in the *Washington Post*, there is now a frantic campaign to overturn the UN's [United Nations'] "Goldstone Report" into

Daud Abdullah, "Defending the Indefensible," *Middle East Monitor*, April 7, 2011. www.middleeastmonitor.org.uk. Reproduced with permission.

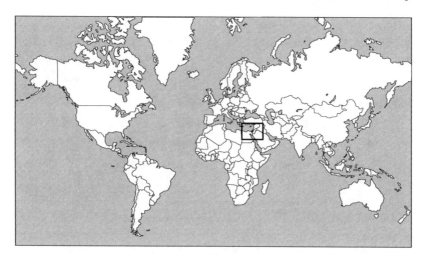

Israel's 2008/9 war against the people of Gaza. [Richard Goldstone, a South African who led a UN investigation into the
2008–2009 Gaza war, co-authored a report that suggested that
Israel may have committed war crimes. In 2011, he wrote an
op-ed partly retracting these accusations.] Leading the charge
is a legion of columnists, public relations handlers, apologists
and spin doctors intent on proving Israeli innocence of all
charges contained in the report. Despite his established record
for balanced analyses, the *Guardian*'s Jonathan Freedland surprisingly made an uncharacteristic threadbare contribution
headed, "Where's the Goldstone report into Sri Lanka, Congo,
Darfur—Britain?"

## Sri Lanka, the Congo, Sudan

The article attempts to make three points: that Israel did not
"intentionally target" civilians during the conflict but Hamas
did; that war crimes are committed elsewhere so why single
out Israel; and negate the centrality of Palestine in the uprisings across the Middle East and North Africa.

The insinuation that there has been no international action to prosecute persons suspected for war crimes in the
three trouble spots Freedland names is a gross misrepresenta-

tion of the facts. In November 2010, Sri Lanka's President Mahinda Rajapaksa was forced, like several Israeli war crime suspects before him, to cancel a visit to Britain amid fears that he might be arrested for war crimes under the principle of universal jurisdiction.

In the cases of the Congo and Sudan, it is well known that the International Criminal Court (ICC) has issued warrants for the arrests of Bosco Ntaganda, the former alleged Deputy Chief of the Patriotic Forces for the Liberation of the Congo (FPLC), and Sudan's President Omar [al-]Bashir.

---

*Israel has never been challenged or censured for any of its notorious crimes.*

---

In an interesting apparently unrelated development, a lawsuit will begin this week [in April 2011] in a British court with five elderly Kenyans taking on the UK [United Kingdom] government over torture allegations during the Mau Mau rebellion against British rule between 1952 and 1960. Will such a case ever take place in Israel? How many Palestinians have been able to launch such legal action in Israel? Every attempt to take Israel to task in a European court has been met with protection and subterfuge from Israel's friends, Britain included.

On the central issue of the Goldstone Report, Freedland wrote with dismissive abandon as if it was a personal undertaking of the retired South African, pro-Israel, judge. He gives scant recognition to the fact that this was a UN-accredited investigation. When he does, he reviles the UN Human Rights Council (UNHRC) claiming that it has "only one rapporteur whose mandate never expires". If this was meant as a below-the-belt swipe at Richard Falk, the incumbent rapporteur, it too was simply not true; Falk was preceded by another legal expert, John Dugard, who has said that Goldstone's op-ed in the *Washington Post* "makes strange reading".

Freedland plays the victim card, claiming that Israel has, for years, been hounded maliciously by the UNHRC. The reality is very different; Israel has never been challenged or censured for any of its notorious crimes. The recent farce in the Security Council concerning its West Bank settlements speaks volumes. Fourteen members of the body agreed that the settlements are illegal based on a resolution sponsored by 130 member states of the UN, then along comes America and vetoes the resolution. Protection and subterfuge.

## A Mockery of Justice

This latest abuse of a Security Council veto makes a mockery of the principle of justice and the rule of law. [Ambassador] Susan Rice said the veto was not indicative of any support for the settlements. Perhaps that is true, but the US veto sent a message to the world that America will sacrifice the principles of its founding fathers in order to protect Israel from legal accountability for its crimes. In 2004, the US was no less generous in its patronage of the Zionist state when it defied the unanimous will of 14 judges in the International Court of Justice by abstaining on a vote which also declared Israeli settlements in the occupied Palestinian territories to be illegal.

The overarching reality about the Gaza conflict, which the Goldstone Report failed to highlight, is that Israel, the occupying state, launched a war on the Palestinians in Gaza, an occupied people. The two protagonists were not the same, morally or legally, let alone militarily. For more than 60 years Israel has maintained its military dominance over the people in the land it occupies, dictating and disrupting almost every aspect of their daily lives. Lavished with the most advanced and destructive weapons by the US, Israel has attempted to quell Palestinian aspirations for freedom in many ways. None have succeeded. In fact, the Gaza conflict confirmed Israel's inability to accomplish this task. In this asymmetrical military and political conflict they have even been denied the right to self-defence and freedom, so in the face of such vicious serial attacks, should the Palestinians lie down and die like sacrificial lambs to placate the occupier?

The same do-gooders who deny the right of self-defence to the Palestinians stand on their moral high horse and proclaim the need to arm the Libyan opposition to defend themselves against the brutality of their oppressor. [In 2011, North Atlantic Treaty Organization nations aided Libyan rebels against Libyan leader Muammar Gaddafi.] Suggest to these do-gooders, aka Western leaders in Paris, London, Berlin and Washington [D.C.], that they should arm the Palestinians, then watch them squirm in their equivocation. Try to convince them that if the Palestinians had the same precision weapons as the Israelis it would reduce the chances of civilian casualties ("collateral damage"), and watch their reaction. In 1949, Israel's first Prime Minister, David Ben-Gurion, said that his country's security problem is "utterly unique and [without] parallel among the nations". Politicians in the West, ever mindful of the Israel lobby's ability to deliver campaign funds and votes, have swallowed that lie ever since.

---

*The overarching reality about the Gaza conflict . . . is that Israel, the occupying state, launched a war on the Palestinians in Gaza, an occupied people.*

---

The shameful bottom line in this latest debate about the Goldstone Report is that the world couldn't care less whether a generation of Palestinian children in the Gaza Strip suffer from multiple trauma and psychological disorders because of Israel's relentless night bombings and terrifying low-flying aircraft breaking the sound barrier. Palestinians in Gaza have almost become non-people. Moreover, have Israel's apologists in Western capitals ever considered a no-fly zone over the Gaza Strip? Of course not; even though this is the longest-running

"The Goldstone Report on Gaza," cartoon by Patrick Chappatte, in *Le Temps* (Geneva), October 17, 2009, www.globecartoon.com. Copyright © Chappatte 2009 in *Le Temps* (Geneva)—www.globecartoon.com.

conflict in the world, whose impact cannot be grasped by the numbers killed but by the millions of lives it affects well beyond the region.

Surprisingly for such a prominent journalist on a left-of-centre newspaper, Jonathan Freedland's article echoes far-right Israeli politician Avigdor Lieberman and other Israel officials: Namely, that Palestine is not the central issue for the people of the region. Just five years ago, Kofi Annan, the former UN secretary-general begged to differ:

"We might like to think of the Arab-Israeli conflict as just one regional conflict among many. But it is not. No other conflict carries such a powerful symbolic and emotional charge among people far removed from the battlefield."

More recently, Egypt's Foreign Minister, Nabil el-Arabi, was even more specific after his meeting with a Hamas delegation in Cairo. The humanitarian situation in Gaza, he said, is a priority for revolutionary Egypt. Despite their empty treasury and incalculable domestic challenges the message could not be any clearer.

It is right that the emerging orders in Egypt, Tunisia and elsewhere should first clear the decks, rid themselves of the humiliating legacies of the Arab-Zionists and then address the issue of Palestine. For decades the Western-backed dictatorships have stood against their people in favour of Israel, maintained its blockade of Gaza, sowed division among the Palestinians and isolated them. There is no doubt that once the last of these double agents have been weeded out Palestine will return to the political front line.

More than any previous generation, the Arab youth who are changing the status quo know that Israel does not only seek to occupy Palestinian and neighbouring lands. It also seeks to crush the aspirations of the region's people for genuine independence and development. They recall that it was Israel who, along with Britain and France, launched the Tripartite attack against revolutionary Egypt in 1956 when it sought to nationalise the Suez Canal. Today, regional despots like Gaddafi use Israel as cover to justify their vile tyranny. On March 7 [2011], he told France 24 TV network that his violent crackdown on opposition protesters is akin to Israel's efforts to defend itself from extremism during its war on Gaza. It has since transpired that he has been receiving military aid from Israel. As a result, Fatah [a Palestinian political party] has launched an investigation into its controversial operative, Muhammad Dahlan, for transhipping Israeli weapons to Gaddafi.

## Israel Will Answer for Its Crimes

Meanwhile, Israel and its backers in Washington will continue to claim that this "Arab spring" offers a great opportunity for peace in Palestine. No one is impressed, not even the PLO [Palestine Liberation Organization] which recognizes and accepts Israel on 78% of historic Palestine. For two decades the PLO has negotiated with Israel; all it got in return was the loss of ever more land. The PLO knows that the sentiment on the

"Arab street" across the region is that negotiations have become an end in themselves and not the path to freedom.

In the end, that strange op-ed by the chairman of the UN fact-finding mission, Judge Richard Goldstone, will not change the collective findings of the eminent team of investigators; Goldstone was, after all, but one of four on the commission. Apart from anything else, if there was no credible case for prosecuting Israeli war criminals, US envoy George Mitchell would not have browbeaten the Palestinian negotiator Saeb Erekat in order to avoid the Goldstone Report going to the International Criminal Court. Mitchell told Erekat on 21 October 2009, "You can go for a public statement. The ICC is a different thing." Likewise, if there was no case to answer, the Zionist lobby in Britain would not have gone to such great lengths to ensure that the UK changes its laws on universal jurisdiction.

---

*For two decades the [Palestine Liberation Organization] has negotiated with Israel; all it got in return was the loss of ever more land.*

---

The simple fact of the matter is that Israel has plenty to answer for in the court of world opinion; it has displayed contempt for international laws and conventions for decades and it can only be a matter of time before it is brought before the International Criminal Court to answer for its crimes. The Palestinian quest for justice will continue because Israel's friends cannot defend the indefensible forever.

# The Blockade of Gaza Is Inhumane and Must Cease

*International Federation for Human Rights*

*The International Federation for Human Rights (FIDH) is a nongovernmental federation for human rights organizations. In the following viewpoint, the FIDH reports that Israel has promised to ease restrictions on movement in Gaza. However, the FIDH says, the lockdown continues to severely restrict economic activity as well as the movement of medical supplies and humanitarian aid. The blockade of Gaza, FIDH argues, violates human rights standards and international law. It concludes that restrictions on humanitarian aid and other necessary supplies must be lifted.*

As you read, consider the following questions:

1. Name one measure that Israel announced was meant to ease the blockade of Gaza.

2. How many trucks does FIDH say have left Gaza since Israel agreed to ease the blockade?

3. At what point does the FIDH say that Israel began to intensify restrictions, and why did it do so?

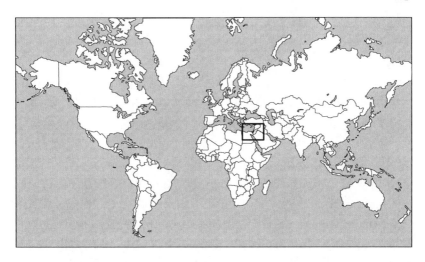

On June 20, 2010, following concerted international pressure, the Government of Israel announced a set of measures to 'ease' its illegal blockade of the Gaza Strip. This included:

- Publishing a list of items not permitted into Gaza and allowing all other items to enter;

- Expanding and accelerating the inflow of construction materials for international projects;

- Expanding operations at the crossings and opening more crossings as more processing capacity becomes necessary and security conditions allow;

- Streamlining entry/exit permits for medical and humanitarian reasons and for aid workers;

- Facilitating the movement of people in additional ways as conditions and security allow.

## Fully Lift the Blockade

Many in the international community . . . expressed hopes that this would lead to a major change and alleviate the plight of the Palestinian civilian population in Gaza. However, five months later, there are few signs of real improvement on the ground as the 'ease' has left foundations of the illegal blockade policy intact. In order to have a positive impact on the daily lives of the 1.5 million Palestinians in Gaza, half of whom are children, Israel must fully lift its blockade of the Gaza Strip.

While the Government of Israel committed to expand and accelerate the inflow of construction materials for international projects, it has so far only approved 7 per cent of the building plan for UNRWA's [United Nations Relief and Works Agency's] projects in Gaza, and of that 7 per cent only a small fraction of the necessary construction material has been allowed to enter for projects including schools and health centres. In fact, the UN reports that Gaza requires 670,000 truckloads of construction material, while only an average of 715 of these truckloads have been received per month since the 'easing' was announced.

While the Government of Israel committed to expand operations at the crossings and to open further crossings as necessary, and has indeed undertaken an expansion of the operations at the limited Kerem Shalom crossing, the main Karni commercial crossing stands idle. While the Government of Israel committed to more than double operations at the Karni conveyor belt, the operations there have in fact decreased since the 'easing'. Exports remain banned and except for the humanitarian activity of exporting a small amount of strawberries, not a single truck has left Gaza since the easing.

Although there has been a significant increase in the amount of food stuffs entering Gaza, many humanitarian items, including vital water equipment, that are not on the Israeli restricted list continue to receive no permits. Two-thirds of Gaza's factories report they have received none or only some of the raw materials they need to recommence operations. As a result, 39 per cent of Gaza residents remain unemployed and unable to afford the new goods in the shops. Without raw materials and the chance to export, Gaza's businesses

## Selected Items Permitted and Prohibited in Israel's Blockade of the Gaza Strip, as of May 6, 2010

| Permitted | Prohibited |
| --- | --- |
| Animal feed, hay | Canned fruit, dried fruit |
| Aniseed, cinnamon, black pepper | Chicken hatcheries, chickens |
| Cartons for transporting chicks | Coriander, ginger, nutmeg |
| Chemical fertilizer and pesticide | Donkeys, horses, goats, cattle |
| Clothes | Fabric for clothing |
| Fresh fruit, frozen fruit | Fishing rods, ropes for fishing |
| Frozen fish | Fresh meat |
| Frozen meat and vegetables | Musical instruments |
| Medicine and medical equipment | Newspapers |
| Rice, chickpeas, beans | Seeds and nuts |
| Wood for doors and windows | Wood for construction |

Source: Gisha

TAKEN FROM: *The Economist*, "Israel's Blockade of the Gaza Strip: Trade Off," June 1, 2010. www.economist.com.

are unable to compete with the cheaper, newly imported goods. This economic development leaves 80 per cent of the population dependent upon international aid.

More Palestinian businesspeople than before have been allowed to leave Gaza, but ordinary Gaza residents are still denied access to their friends and family, and to educational opportunities in the West Bank, East Jerusalem and abroad.

*39 per cent of Gaza residents remain unemployed and unable to afford the new goods in the shops.*

## Additional Sanctions

While restrictions on access to and from Gaza date back to the 1990s, these restrictions were intensified leading to the current blockade after Hamas [a militant Islamic group and political party] took control of the Strip in June 2007. The Israeli Security Cabinet declared Gaza a 'hostile entity' and decided to impose additional sanctions restricting the passage of goods, fuel and people. Israel has a duty to protect its citizens from security threats and the measures it uses to do so must conform to international humanitarian and human rights law. This includes its legal obligation as an occupying power to protect the safety, rights and needs of the occupied civilian population. The government of Israel holds the position that the restrictions and procedures are part of legitimate warfare. However, the International Committee of the Red Cross has recently confirmed that the blockade constitutes a collective punishment of the entire civilian population of Gaza and is in clear violation of international humanitarian law.

---

*The blockade constitutes a collective punishment of the entire civilian population of Gaza and is in clear violation of international humanitarian law.*

---

Following the Israeli announcement of steps to 'ease' the blockade, international attention shifted to the Israeli-Palestinian negotiations and the pressure from the international community to lift the blockade was also eased. The current approach risks perpetuating what is an unacceptable situation and fails to recognise that there cannot be a just and durable resolution of the Israeli-Palestinian conflict without an end to the isolation and punishment of people in Gaza. The Government of Israel and parts of the international community remain reluctant to fully lift the blockade as long as Hamas holds power in Gaza. Yet, upholding the rights and needs of civilians in Gaza must not be conditional on other political objectives. Civilians in Gaza cannot wait until the Israeli-Palestinian negotiations are concluded.

Lifting the blockade of Gaza remains a legal, economic and political imperative for those seeking a lasting resolution to the Israeli-Palestinian conflict. The time for credible and effective action is now.

# The Blockade of Gaza
# Is Justified

*Allison Kaplan Sommer*

*Allison Kaplan Sommer is an American-born writer living in Israel; she is a former writer for the* Jerusalem Post *and a former editor of Pajamas Media. In the following viewpoint, she argues that without the Gaza blockade, Hamas would fire rockets into southern Israel. She also notes that removing the blockade without concessions would strengthen Hamas. This would hurt the Palestinian Authority, which, as a result, is not eager to see the blockade lifted, according to Sommer.*

As you read, consider the following questions:

1. Who is Galid Shalit, and how does he affect Israeli attitudes toward the Gaza blockade, according to Sommer?

2. Why does Sommer suggest that Egypt is not eager to have the blockade lifted?

3. What goods and services does the *Los Angeles Times* report as being available in Gaza despite the blockade?

There couldn't be much more pressure on Israel at the moment [June 2010] to end the blockade on Gaza.

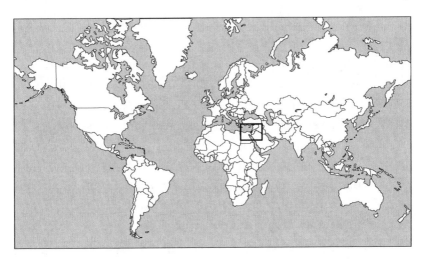

## Pressure Mounts

Following the traumatic flotilla raid,[1] the international community has determined that Israel deserves to do penance for the events on the *[Mavi] Marmara* by lifting its "siege" on Gaza. The pressure is coming from all sides, though most heavily from Europe. Spanish Prime Minister [José Luis Rodríguez] Zapatero has decided that the European Union has to "exert strong diplomatic pressure" on Israel to stop blockading Gaza. Egypt's Amr Moussa, the current head of the Arab League, made a rare visit to Gaza and declared that the League would go to the UN [United Nations] to demand Israel lift the blockade. Even the [US President Barack] Obama administration has joined in, calling the blockade "unsustainable." Internally, Israeli human rights group B'Tselem says the Gazan economy is "collapsing under the siege."

Israel has serious reasons to oppose opening the Gaza borders. On a security level, it does not want materials to enter Gaza that it has good reason to believe will be used by Hamas as weaponry to attack Israel. But on a political and moral

---

1. On May 31, 2010, the Israeli military boarded ships bringing humanitarian aid to Gaza in an effort to break Israel's blockade. Activists on the ships resisted and nine were killed.

level, there is Gilad Shalit [an Israeli soldier captured by Hamas in 2006 and held captive since]. The central role that Shalit's captivity plays in Israeli public opposition to ending or easing the blockade on Gaza is not fully communicated overseas, but domestically, it dominates. No Israeli government can be seen as handing over important bargaining chips as long as the Israeli soldier remains in enemy hands, as he has for four years in conditions that are in complete violation of international regulations regarding the treatment of prisoners. The Israeli public isn't in the mood to ease up on Hamas as Shalit's human rights are deprived.

And yet, the force of the international pressure is difficult to resist. The [Prime Minister Benjamin] Netanyahu government has made moves to "revamp" the restrictions on goods and movement in and out of Gaza, while at the same time declaring the restrictions will not be lifted completely.

---

*[Israel] does not want materials to enter Gaza that it has good reason to believe will be used by Hamas as weaponry to attack Israel.*

---

## Arab Support

On the surface, it seems as if the Arab world is united in its call to "Free Gaza." However, while leaders of the Palestinian Authority [PA] in the West Bank publicly chastise Israel for maintaining the "Gaza prison," some sources whisper a different story.

According to a report in *Haaretz*, PA President Mahmoud Abbas has let it be known that he isn't very happy about the prospect of a "Free Gaza," and he even let President Obama know it at their meeting last week [in June 2010]:

European diplomats updated by the White House on the talks said that Abbas had stressed to Obama the need of opening the border crossings into the Gaza Strip and the easing of the siege, but only in ways that do not bolster Hamas.

One of the points that Abbas raised is that the naval blockade imposed by Israel on the Strip should not be lifted at this stage. The European diplomats said Egypt has made it clear to Israel, the U.S, and the European Union that it also opposes the lifting of the naval blockade because of the difficulty in inspecting the ships that would enter and leave the Gaza port.

Abbas told Obama that actions easing the blockage should be done with care and undertaken gradually so it will not be construed as a victory for Hamas. The Palestinian leader also stressed that the population in the Gaza Strip must be supported, and that pressure should be brought to bear on Israel to allow more goods, humanitarian assistance, and building materials for reconstruction. Abbas, however, said this added aid can be done by opening land crossings and other steps that do not include the lifting of the naval blockade.

The Palestinians immediately slapped a denial on the report, calling it "baseless." But the story has a ring of truth to it.

---

*Egypt has made it clear that it does not want boats freely sailing in and out of Gaza's port any more than Israel does.*

---

After all, much of the justification for the blockade policy had been based in it strengthening the PA as opposed to Hamas, following Hamas' violent ouster of the PA in 2007. While it may not be politically correct on the Palestinian street to admit it out loud, what is good for Hamas is bad for Fatah [the political party supporting the PA] and the PA. The international support for Hamas post-flotilla hurts their position.

It also puts Egypt in a more precarious position. The Egyptian authorities, like their West Bank counterparts, affect an outward solidarity with their suffering Arab brothers. Yet they are far from enthusiastic about having open borders with a Hamas-controlled Gaza. Israel has not exactly had to twist their arm to get them to keep a close watch on the Rafah crossing on the Gaza-Egyptian border.

The pressure following the flotilla incident forced Egypt to open the Rafah border, albeit in a limited manner. But the press reports that, behind closed diplomatic doors, Egypt has made it clear that it does not want boats freely sailing in and out of Gaza's port any more than Israel does [from a June 14, 2010, article in the *Australian*]:

> Egypt has told the U.S. and European countries that the maritime blockade should not be lifted because it would be too difficult to inspect ships entering Gaza to ensure they do not carry weaponry. Egypt regards Hamas as a dangerous neighbor, and fears the Islamic group's contacts with the outlawed Muslim Brotherhood [an opposition Islamic group] inside Egypt.

Hamas was clearly feeling its suddenly powerful position vis-à-vis the PA and Egypt on Sunday, when it boldly rebuffed attempts to revive an Egyptian-led reconciliation effort with Fatah—which many believe is essential to end the blockade. The *Jerusalem Post* reports:

> Hamas has rejected Palestinian Authority President Mahmoud Abbas's offer to dispatch a Fatah delegation to the Gaza Strip to discuss ways of ending the power struggle between the two parties, Fatah officials in Ramallah said over the weekend.
>
> Hamas's refusal to receive the delegation comes as the two sides face growing pressure from several Arab and Islamic countries to patch up their differences so as to pave the way for the lifting of the blockade on the Gaza Strip.

Presumably, in the current atmosphere, Hamas is confident that it can get the blockade lifted without making any concessions, so it is not quite as desperate as the rest of the world to ease the conditions in Gaza.

So what are those conditions exactly?

## The Gaza Blockade Is Not the Main Issue

One interesting consequence of the Gaza flotilla crisis is the way it has brought mainstream media into Gaza to report the situation on the ground more extensively than they have done in a long time. The *Los Angeles Times* writes:

> The stores are stocked with food, electronics, furniture, and clothing, much of it smuggled from Egypt through illegal tunnels. Cafes offer espresso and croissants. A shipment of 2010 Hyundai sedans recently arrived. Now that school is out for the summer, families are flocking to the beach to eat ice cream and barbecue.

To be sure, the description is given together with a description of undersupplied hospitals and children suffering and dying because they are not permitted out of the Strip to reach hospitals that can offer them surgery they cannot obtain locally.

> *Despite the international demonization of their intentions towards the people of Gaza, the vast majority of Israelis would be more than happy to make [freedom] available to them.*

Even Taghreed al-Khodary—a Gaza resident herself who served for years as the *New York Times* correspondent there, and is now living abroad as a fellow at the Carnegie Institute—admits that the political and symbolic value of the flotilla efforts far outweigh anything they contribute to Gaza on a practical level:

The people in Gaza are not in need of humanitarian aid. They need the Israeli blockade to end, access and exposure to the outside world, a formal economy, and freedom.

Despite the international demonization of their intentions towards the people of Gaza, the vast majority of Israelis would be more than happy to make all of this available to them. But they need to believe that such a move wouldn't be construed as an invitation to once again rain rockets on southern Israel.

Most importantly, they insist Gilad Shalit be given the opportunity to enjoy "access and exposure to the outside world" and freedom, as well.

# Periodical and Internet Sources Bibliography

*The following articles have been selected to supplement the diverse views presented in this chapter.*

| | |
|---|---|
| Amnesty International UK | "Israeli Campaign to Avoid Accountability for Gaza War Crimes Must Be Rejected," April 5, 2011. www.amnesty.org.uk. |
| Adam Davidson | "Hamas: Government or Terrorist Organization?," National Public Radio, December 6, 2006. www.npr.org. |
| *Economist* | "Hamas Hangs On," March 31, 2010. |
| Steven Erlanger | "A Gaza War Full of Traps and Trickery," *New York Times*, January 10, 2009. |
| Sheera Frenkel | "Israeli Document: Gaza Blockade Isn't About Security," McClatchy, June 9, 2010. www.mcclatchydc.com. |
| Glenn Greenwald | "Majority of Israelis Want to Negotiate with Hamas," *Salon*, February 27, 2008. www.salon.com. |
| *Jerusalem Post* | "Barak: If Hamas Stops Firing from Gaza, We'll Stop Firing," April 10, 2011. |
| Rashid Khalidi | "What You Don't Know About Gaza," *New York Times*, January 7, 2009. |
| Stuart Robinowitz | "Human Rights Watch Owes Israel an Apology," *Daily Beast*, April 12, 2011. www.thedailybeast.com. |
| *Room for Debate* (blog) | "Rethinking the Gaza Blockade," June 1, 2010. http://roomfordebate.blogs.nytimes.com. |
| Michael Weiss | "Hamas Isn't the IRA," *Slate*, September 17, 2010. www.slate.com. |

GLOBAL VIEWPOINTS

## CHAPTER 3

# Israel and the West Bank

# Israeli Settlements in the West Bank Should Cease

*Jonathan Kay*

*Jonathan Kay is managing editor and columnist for Canada's National Post. In the following viewpoint, he argues that Palestinian president Mahmoud Abbas is serious about peace and that peace talks between Palestinians and Israel are substantive. Kay says that to achieve peace Abbas will have to make real concessions and risk personal attacks by hard-line Islamists. Given that, Kay says, Israeli president Benjamin Netanyahu should meet Abbas halfway and freeze settlement construction in the West Bank during the peace negotiations.*

As you read, consider the following questions:

1. By whom was Anwar Sadat killed, and how is this relevant to Mahmoud Abbas, according to Kay?
2. How does Kay identify the "right of return"?
3. At what rate has the economy of the West Bank been growing, and to what does Kay attribute this growth?

It is fashionable to dismiss the current round of Middle East peace negotiations [September 2010] as pointless diplomatic kabuki. But it's not. Palestinian Authority (PA) President Mahmoud Abbas—unlike his predecessor, Yasser Arafat—seems genuinely interested in transforming the West Bank

Jonathan Kay, "Jonathan Kay on the Middle East: Stop Building Settlements," *The National Post*, September 16, 2010. Reproduced with permission.

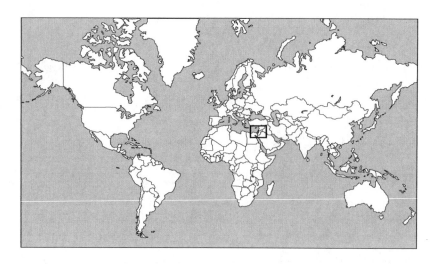

into a normal, peaceable society. (Indeed, to a great extent, he already has.) And while Israeli Prime Minister Benjamin Netanyahu routinely is described as "hawkish," he is not delusional: He realizes that the only long-term solution to the Israeli-Palestinian problem is a two-state solution; and that, until one is achieved, the spectacle of Palestinian suffering will strengthen the hand of unstable regional warmongers, from Beirut [Lebanon] to Damascus [Syria] to Tehran [Iran].

## Productive and Serious Talks

Moreover, both sides have learned from past diplomatic failures, and have avoided the mistake of pushing divisive issues off into the future. They have elected instead to tackle the most difficult negotiations—over borders, refugees, settlements and the status of Jerusalem—before announcing interim agreements. This week, U.S. envoy George Mitchell declared that these peace talks are more productive and serious, in their early stages at least, than those he brokered in Northern Ireland.

Critics who say that Mr. Abbas is not serious about peace should re-read Khaled Abu Toameh's column, which appeared in Thursday's *National Post*. As Mr. Toameh argued, the mere fact that the PA President is sitting down to talk with the Israelis means he has a bull's-eye on his head—the mark carried by every Arab "traitor" who commits the crime of negotiating with Zionists. Former Egyptian President Anwar Sadat, who traded land for peace, could attest to that—if he hadn't been killed by Islamists.

As the talks proceed, things will only get more difficult for Mr. Abbas. That is because everyone involved knows that no peace deal can be reached unless the Palestinians give up the "right of return," which would allow millions of descendants of Palestinian refugees to flood Israel's pre-1967 boundaries, and thereby hopelessly destabilize the Jewish state. For years, Palestinians have been fed the myth that one day they would be permitted to march back into villages and homes once owned by their great-grandparents. Many still make a fetish of their old house keys, and name sections of refugee camps after Israeli neighbourhoods they have never seen, but which they imagine to be their true home.

If a peace agreement is reached, Mr. Abbas will be the one to tell these people that their dream is over, that they will have to build new lives in the West Bank or Gaza. He will also have to cross Hamas' ultimate red line and recognize Israel as a legitimate, and Jewish, state. Not an enviable task.

*Mr. Netanyahu should ... pledge to an indefinite freeze on new settlement construction during the peace talks.*

## Peace Is Worth It

But the prize of peace is worth it—for Palestinians and Jews alike. This year, the economy in the West Bank has been growing at the shockingly high annualized rate of 9%, according to the International Monetary Fund—primarily because the PA has almost entirely wiped out the local terror apparatus, and Israel has responded by easing blockades. This is just a taste of

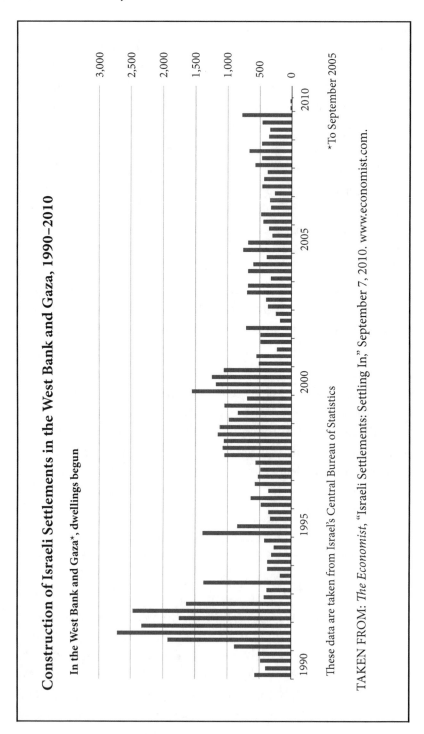

## Construction of Israeli Settlements in the West Bank and Gaza, 1990–2010

In the West Bank and Gaza*, dwellings begun

These data are taken from Israel's Central Bureau of Statistics

*To September 2005

TAKEN FROM: *The Economist*, "Israeli Settlements: Settling In," September 7, 2010. www.economist.com.

the prosperity that will come with a true and lasting peace. The transformation of Palestinian society from an anti-Semitic martyrdom cult to a modern, market-oriented nation-state could be Mr. Abbas' legacy.

Mr. Netanyahu should consider his own legacy, as well. For years, the world has had no more articulate advocate for Israel and its right to defend itself. The Israeli Prime Minister often speaks in the soaring language of principles and rights—including Israel's right to create defensible borders and expand existing settlements in the West Bank. Only grudgingly did he agree to a 10-month freeze on new settlement construction—a period that is set to expire later this month. As things stand, there is no indication that he will extend the moratorium. Mr. Abbas has said his team will walk out of peace talks if he doesn't.

Mr. Netanyahu should relent on this issue, and pledge to an indefinite freeze on new settlement construction during the peace talks. Israel's supporters have all sorts of perfectly valid arguments about why, in theory, the Israeli Prime Minister should have no obligation to make such a pledge. But negotiations aren't conducted in theory. They're conducted with other human beings—in this case, Palestinians whose entire political narrative is based on an obsessive fear of Jews taking land they regard as theirs. The ongoing construction of new settlements is the steel and wood embodiment of those fears.

It would not be a sign of appeasement or weakness on Mr. Netanyahu's part to recognize that fact. Indeed, history would remember him kindly for his courage.

# Israeli Settlements Are Legitimate and Must Be Defended

**Gavriel Queenann**

*Gavriel Queenann is a writer for Israelnationalnews.com. In the following viewpoint, he states that there has been a record increase in the population of Israel's settlements in the West Bank. Despite the attempts of Israel's enemies to discourage their settlement there, Israel believes their communities to be legitimate and will not let fear keep them from defending their settlements in what they consider their homeland. Queenann maintains that the Israeli settlers will not be pushed out of their homes and will defend their communities from their enemy.*

As you read, consider the following questions:

1. According to the viewpoint, how many families have moved into Itamar after the Fogel massacre?
2. According to the Interior Ministry, what was the percentage of growth in births and residents moving into the Itamar region?
3. As stated in the viewpoint, to what does the growth in the population of the Itamar region bear witness?

Gavriel Queenann, "Itamar Answers Tragedy with Growth," www.israelnationalnews .com, November 18, 2011. Reproduced with permission.

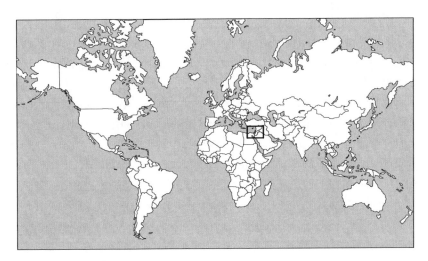

The horrific Fogel massacre in Itamar raised fears communities in Judea and Samaria near hostile Arab villages would have difficulty attracting new residents—but the opposite has proven itself true.

## Record Increase

Just eight months after the tragedy that outraged and shocked the nation of Israel, Itamar's community secretariat says there have seen a record increase of families move into the community.

*According to the Interior Ministry, that Judea and Samaria's population growth from both births and residents moving into the region, is 10%.*

Since the massacre, they say, 12 families have moved to Itamar. This was compared to just 6 families moving into the community in the year preceding the murders—a clear 100% increase in the community's growth rate.

Moshe Goldsmith, chairman of Itamar's secretariat, says the trend represents the Israeli public's true spirit in answering the murders.

"I feel this has two main reasons," Goldsmith said. "One is that in general, Itamar is a community with a lot to give. There's a good company and a good atmosphere—it's just a good place to live."

"The other reason is that people come filled with fire for the Zionist mission; they want to show our enemies they cannot weaken us—and that the murders will bring no long-term benefit. On the contrary, they reinforce our resolve."

---

*Contributing to Itamar's growth is the strength of its yeshiva, of whose 80 students ten have settled in the community.*

---

## Strength and Faith of the Residents

Goldsmith reported Itamar was at full occupancy due to the unprecedented growth rate, but noted seven houses are available for sale.

Samaria Regional Council head Gershon Mesika praised the residents of Itamar, "We all admire the great strength and enormous faith of the wonderful residents of Itamar. Israel can be proud of having such people."

Mesika added, according to the Interior Ministry, that Judea and Samaria's population growth from both births and residents moving into the region, is 10%—the highest in the country for two consecutive years.

Contributing to Itamar's growth is the strength of its yeshiva, of whose 80 students ten have settled in the community.

Rabbi Avichai Ronsky, head of the yeshiva in Itamar, gave his explanation for the phenomenon: "We have seen how we are all words of the Torah. The more they are afflicted by him the more they multiply and refuse to break."

"The growth here bears witness to the determination of Israel's public to hold onto Judea and Samaria—especially

---

## Some Palestinians Praise the Murder of Settlers

Sawsan Al-Barghouti, a columnist for a website affiliated with Hamas, called the Itamar murders [in which five settlers, including children, were killed] a "heroic act": "The heroic act in Nablus struck stunning blows, the first of which was against the supporters of coexistence [between the Palestinians] and the Jews on the holy and proud land of Palestine. Stability, security, freedom and independence cannot prevail as long as there are recruits [in Palestine], each and every one armed from head to toe and supported by their thieving and plundering government. . . .

"This heroic deed, and ones like it, have successfully sabotaged the Arab initiative [i.e., the Saudi Arab peace initiative], which is not worth a single glance."

*Middle East Media Research Institute,*
*"Palestinian Reactions to the Itamar Murder, Part II:*
*Praise by Hamas; Condemnation in PA—Amid Accusations*
*That Israel Is Exploiting the Murders for Political Aims,"*
*Special Dispatch No. 3679, March 18, 2011. www.memriblog.org.*

---

when our enemies are trying to harm us. We understand the murders were motivated by our enemies trying to discourage us from maintaining our foothold in our homeland—they will not succeed."

David and Einat Cohen, a young couple from Giv'at Ze'ev, moved into the community less than a month ago. A student at the Itamar yeshiva, Cohen and his wife have a daughter less than a year old.

"We decided fear would not rule our lives," explains Cohen. "In the end, it is good a town to live in. The first night

... it was hard to sleep, but we have great support from our community, the yeshiva, and our parents. We know we've made the right choice."

"People here do not base their lives on the murders," Cohen added. "Life is stronger than death."

# Israel's Restrictions on Movement in the West Bank Are Inhumane

## Amnesty International

*Amnesty International is an international nongovernmental organization devoted to ending human rights abuses. In the following viewpoint, the organization argues that restrictions on movement in the West Bank are inhumane. The organization says that the restrictions sometimes result in deaths because Palestinians have to wait to reach hospitals or medical care. Amnesty International argues, in addition, that the barriers and checkpoints within the occupied territory are illegal and that the Israeli wall that annexes Palestinian territory violates international law.*

As you read, consider the following questions:

1. What is the size of the West Bank, according to Amnesty International?

2. According to Amnesty International, what is the Green Line?

3. Who is 'Adel 'Omar, and how did the Israeli blockades affect him?

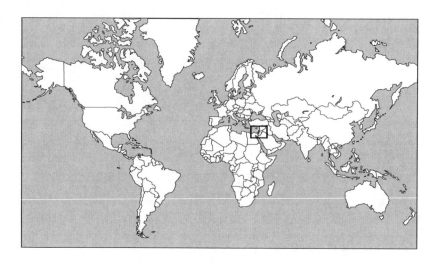

Khaled Daud Faqih was just six months old when he died on 8 March 2007 at an Israeli army checkpoint. His parents, from the village of Kafr Ain, had been trying to rush their baby to the nearby hospital in Ramallah in the West Bank, but were forced to wait at the checkpoint by Israeli soldiers. His father Daud, a teacher, told Amnesty International:

> My son Khaled was having difficulty breathing. I called a neighbour who has a car and with my wife and the baby we set off immediately for the hospital in Ramallah. It was quicker than waiting for an ambulance to come all the way to the village. It was just before half past midnight. Khaled had previously had attacks like this and we took him to hospital and there he was put under the oxygen tent and he always got better.
>
> We arrived at the Atara checkpoint at 12:45 a.m. From there it was another 10 minutes to the hospital. The soldiers stopped us. There were five soldiers. I told them that my baby was sick and urgently needed to get to the hospital in Ramallah. I spoke to them in Hebrew. They asked for our IDs. The driver and I gave ours but my wife had left hers at home in the hurry. I told the soldiers and they said we could not pass without her ID. I begged them to let us pass.

They looked in the car and saw that there was nothing and that the baby had problems breathing and his limbs were trembling. I told the soldiers that every minute, every second mattered; that the baby needed oxygen urgently. They told us to wait and I kept pleading with them. Then the baby died. It was 1:05 a.m. I told the soldiers. They shone a torch into the car and saw that the baby was not moving anymore and told us that we could pass. We drove to the hospital anyway. There it was confirmed that Khaled had died.

## Unlawful and Deadly

Such cases are neither new nor rare. The hundreds of checkpoints and blockades which every day force long detours and delays on Palestinians trying to get to work, school or hospital have for years limited their access to essential health services and caused medical complications, births at checkpoints and even death.

The West Bank, the focus of this [viewpoint], is a relatively small territory—130 kilometres from north to south and 65 kilometres from east to west at its widest point; 5,600 square kilometres in total. It is crisscrossed by a web of Israeli military checkpoints and blockades—some 550—and a winding 700-kilometre fence/wall which runs from north to south, encircling Palestinian villages as well as whole neighbourhoods in and around East Jerusalem.

> *The hundreds of checkpoints and blockades . . . have for years limited [Palestinians'] access to essential health services and caused medical complications, births at checkpoints and even death.*

The Israeli authorities contend that this regime of closures and restrictions is necessary to prevent Palestinians from entering Israel to carry out suicide bombings and other attacks. However, virtually all the checkpoints, gates, blocked roads and most of the fence/wall are located *inside* the West Bank—*not between* Israel and the West Bank. They curtail or prevent movement between Palestinian towns and villages, splitting and isolating Palestinian communities, separating Palestinians from their agricultural land, hampering access to work, schools, health facilities and relatives, and destroying the Palestinian economy. The fence/wall itself, located as it is inside occupied territory, is unlawful, according to the International Court of Justice (ICJ).

The stringent restrictions on movement imposed for years by the Israeli authorities on more than two million Palestinians who live in the West Bank are unlawful as they are disproportionate, discriminatory and violate the right to freedom of movement. The restrictions are imposed on all Palestinians *because* they are Palestinians and in order to benefit the Israeli settlers whose presence in the occupied West Bank violates international law. They should be lifted now.

## The Fence/Wall Violates Freedoms

The 700-kilometre fence/wall that Israel is building through the West Bank, from north to south and through parts of Jerusalem, is causing massive long-term damage to Palestinian life and is undermining the ability of those living in dozens of villages and communities to realise a wide range of their human rights.

More than half of the length of the fence/wall has been completed [as of 2007] and work is proceeding on the rest. Already, tens of thousands of olive and other trees and areas of fertile agricultural land have been uprooted and destroyed, dozens of homes have been demolished, and tens of thousands of Palestinians have been cut off from their land and means of earning a living.

According to the Israeli authorities, the fence/wall is "a defensive measure, designed to block the passage of terrorists, weapons and explosives into the State of Israel. . . ." Its sole purpose, they say, is "to provide security."

However, most of the fence/wall is not being constructed *between* Israel and the West Bank along the Green Line (the 1949 armistice line which separates the State of Israel from the occupied West Bank). Some 80 per cent of it is located on Palestinian land inside the West Bank, separating Palestinian towns, villages, communities and families from each other; cutting off Palestinian farmers from their land; hindering access to education and health care facilities and other essential services; and separating Palestinian communities from reservoirs and sources of clean water.

The Israeli authorities have an obligation to protect the security of those within Israel's borders, including by preventing entry into Israel of people who may constitute a threat to its security. However, such measures must not violate Israel's obligations under international human rights and humanitarian law. Security measures must be necessary, proportionate and non-discriminatory. This may, for example, include the building of fences, walls, barriers or other structures *on* Israeli territory, but not inside the occupied West Bank.

Because of the meandering route of the fence/wall, it is more than double the length of the Green Line. It is a complex structure, 50 to 100 metres in width and including barbed wire, ditches, trace paths and tank patrol lanes on each side as well as additional buffer zones and no-go areas of varying depths. Its route has been designed to encompass more than 50 Israeli settlements, where some 80 per cent of Israeli settlers live, and large areas of land around them. This will create territorial contiguity of these settlements with Israel while cutting the area off from the rest of the West Bank.

## A Violation of International Law

The extent of the negative impact of the fence/wall on Palestinians throughout the West Bank did not become clear until long after much of the damage was done. The creation of a fence/wall in parts of the West Bank was approved by a ministerial committee in 2001 and the route of Phase 1 was approved by the government in June 2002. However, a full map of the planned route was only made public by the Israeli authorities in October 2003—long after construction had begun.

Amnesty International researchers who visited the West Bank between mid-2002 and mid-2003 found that Palestinians whose land was directly affected by the fence/wall had received little or no information from the Israeli authorities. Most had found land seizure orders accompanied by maps pinned to trees or left under stones by the Israeli army in areas where the fence/wall was going to be built. The maps were unclear, generally poor-quality photocopies, and did not contain a scale or other details necessary to establish the exact route of the fence/wall. Only when Israeli army bulldozers began to uproot trees and dig could Palestinians deduce where the fence/wall would be located.

---

*Only when Israeli army bulldozers began to uproot trees and dig could Palestinians deduce where the fence/wall would be located.*

---

The destruction of property by an occupying power is prohibited "except where such destruction is rendered absolutely necessary by military operations"—even with ample forewarning. In fact, "extensive destruction and appropriation of property, not justified by military necessity and carried out unlawfully and wantonly," is a war crime. Furthermore, the seizure of Palestinian land for the fence/wall without adequate notice, consultation and due process of law, amounted to forced eviction—a further violation of international law—and made it virtually impossible for many affected Palestinians to challenge the route of the fence/wall or the appropriation of their land.

For two years after the first phase of the fence/wall was approved by the Israeli government, the Supreme Court rejected all petitions filed by Palestinians objecting to the route of the fence/wall in the West Bank. Only on 30 June 2004, as the Advisory Opinion of the ICJ was about to be announced, did the Supreme Court order that the fence/wall in the Beit Surik area, north of Jerusalem, be rerouted to take in less Palestinian land. However, even this Supreme Court ruling accepted that Palestinian land could be seized, destroyed and cut off from its owners for the benefit of Israeli settlements whose presence in the OPT [Occupied Palestinian Territories] is unlawful. . . .

## Blocked at Every Turn

'Adel 'Omar, aged 21, died on 17 February 2007 after Israeli soldiers delayed his passage at the gate between the village of 'Azzun 'Atma and the nearby town of Qalqilyah. 'Adel 'Omar had been injured in a tractor accident. The village is surrounded by the fence/wall, and the only way out of it is through a gate which closes at 10 p.m. 'Adel arrived at the checkpoint after 10 p.m. and the soldiers did not open the gate for over an hour. He was still alive when he was allowed to pass, but died before he reached the hospital, only a few kilometres from the gate.

Such deaths are not a new phenomenon. Rula 'Ashtiya, for example, was forced to give birth on the ground, on a dirt road by the Beit Furik checkpoint, after Israeli soldiers refused to allow her through the checkpoint in the early morning of 26 August 2003. Her baby girl died soon after. Rula was in labour and was on her way to Nablus hospital, only a few minutes away. The soldiers manning the checkpoint took no notice of her condition and obvious distress, nor of her husband's pleading. They did not ask to check their IDs and simply told them they could not pass. Only after Rula had given birth and her baby had died did the soldiers allow her and her husband and their dead baby to pass through the checkpoint.

---

*Muhammad Fudah ... missed his wedding on 8 Febru-ary 2007 because Israeli soldiers refused him passage at two checkpoints.*

---

It is not possible to know for certain if 'Adel, Rula's baby and other Palestinians who have died on their way to hospital could have been saved if they had not been delayed by Israeli soldiers at checkpoints. What is certain is that they could have reached the hospitals more quickly, which would have given them a better chance of survival. It is also clear that none of these people could have posed a threat to Israel's security as none was trying to enter Israel. All were attempting to travel between their villages and nearby towns within the occupied West Bank.

The checkpoints, closures and other obstacles disrupt all aspects of Palestinian life, including important social and fam-ily events. Muhammad Fudah, for example, missed his wed-ding on 8 February 2007 because Israeli soldiers refused him passage at two checkpoints as he and his wedding party were trying to reach a nearby village where the wedding was to take place. He told Amnesty International:

> I set off from my home in Nur al-Shams refugee camp in Tulkarem with my relatives on the way to my wedding in the village of Beit Lid. It is not far and we had not expected any particular problems at the checkpoints on the way.... However, when we arrived at the Anabta checkpoint, Israeli soldiers there did not let me and several of my young rela-tives pass. No young people from Tulkarem were allowed through. A relative who speaks fluent Hebrew explained to the soldiers that we were on the way to my wedding in Beit Lid; they said we could not go to Beit Lid. So we decided to

travel to another checkpoint, by al-Ras village. However, there too some of my relatives and I were refused passage and were told to go back home to Tulkarem because we would not be allowed to go to Beit Lid.

My relative again explained to the soldiers that we were going to my wedding in Beit Lid but they refused. They said that boys and girls aged between 16 and 30 were not allowed to pass. The Israeli women who monitor checkpoints [Machsom Watch] were there and also spoke to the soldiers but it made no difference. After an hour my other relatives who were young enough or old enough to be allowed to pass went on to Beit Lid and the others and I went back to Tulkarem and then back to Anabta checkpoint. By then it was late and we had to postpone the wedding to the following day. I eventually managed to reach Beit Lid by going on a detour and I did get married.

Machsom Watch—an Israeli women's human rights group—who were at al-Ras checkpoint at the time, recorded the following:

- 13:50: All people (male and female) between the ages of 16 to 30 who are residents of Tulkarem, Nablus and Jenin, and the villages surrounding these towns, are not allowed southward.

- 14:44: A car with a bridegroom arrives at the checkpoint. His wedding is in Beit Lid. However he is from Tulkarem and young and he is told he can't pass through. A relative of his who is from Taibe and who speaks fluent Hebrew, tries to talk to all the soldiers to convince them to let him pass through.

- 14:50: The bus with only women and children who are heading to Beit Lid for the wedding arrives at the checking booth. IDs are checked. Five of the young women, some with young children, are from Tulkarem and are told to leave the bus.

- 14:59: They are not allowed to pass. They get a taxi on the other side of the street to go back home. The bridegroom has still not been allowed through. Aunts, uncles and other relatives are all standing around trying to figure out what to do. The relative from Taibe continues to go from one soldier to the other to ask for help.

- 15:10: The bridegroom is told he cannot go through. He stands to the side.

- 15:37: The bridegroom is sent home.

## Multiplying Checkpoints

The UN [United Nations] Office for the Coordination of Humanitarian Affairs (OCHA) records the number of checkpoints and blockades in the West Bank. In March 2007 there were 549. Of these, 84 were manned checkpoints and 465 were unmanned blockades, such as locked gates, earth mounds or ditches that make roads impassable, cement blocks and other obstacles that block access to roads.

In addition, thousands of temporary checkpoints, known as "flying checkpoints", are set up every year by Israeli army patrols on roads throughout the West Bank for a limited duration—ranging from half an hour to several hours. OCHA recorded 624 flying checkpoints in February 2007 and 455 the previous month. In 2006 a total of 7,090 was recorded.

*When ... general closures are imposed, no movement is allowed for Palestinians through checkpoints into East Jerusalem and Israel ... except for emergencies.*

The number of checkpoints has fluctuated in recent years. In mid to late 2005, when the restrictions of movement imposed by the Israeli army were less stringent than they have generally been since late 2000, there were some 375 permanent checkpoints or blockades, while the number of additional flying checkpoints varied between 260 and 494 a month.

The Israeli army also declares "general closures" in the OPT, usually on the occasion of Israeli national or religious holidays. When such general closures are imposed, no movement is allowed for Palestinians through checkpoints into East Jerusalem and Israel, as well as through other checkpoints between Palestinian areas near Israel, except for emergencies. However, when checkpoints are closed it is difficult and time-consuming for Palestinians to contact the appropriate Israeli army officials to notify them of the emergency and obtain authorization to pass.

# Restrictions on Movement in the West Bank Are Based on Legitimate Israeli Security Needs

## Hila Tene

*Hila Tene is an attorney specializing in human rights issues in the Israeli Ministry of Justice. In the following viewpoint, she writes that restrictions on movement in the West Bank are required by Israeli security needs. She notes that Palestinians in the West Bank have launched repeated and deadly terrorist attacks and that Israel has the right to defend itself. She says that this right has been repeatedly upheld in Israeli courts. She adds that Israel makes every effort to reduce the burden on Palestinians as long as it can do so without endangering Israeli civilians.*

As you read, consider the following questions:

1. When did the second *intifada* break out, and against whom were its attacks directed, according to Justice Aharon Barak?

2. According to Tene, what efforts specifically does Israel make in order to address the medical needs of those in the West Bank?

Hila Tene, "Reference to the Btselem Draft Report Regarding Restrictions on Movement," State of Israel Ministry of Justice, August 5, 2007, pp. 1–9. www.justice.gov.il. Reproduced with permission.

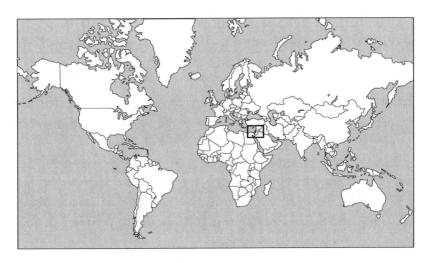

3. What does Tene say is the clear security purpose of barriers on the roads in the West Bank (Judea and Samaria)?

In response to the draft report [by Israeli human rights group B'Tselem on restrictions on movement in the West Bank] which has been received in our office. Our response is as follows . . .

## Coping with Terror

We wish to make clear at the outset that the report in question makes no reference at all to the State of Israel's broader security needs, which are legitimate overall, and form the foundation of the restrictions on movement, as it has been imposed in Judea and Samaria [that is, the West Bank]. The report indicates only that there is a possibility that part of the restrictions on movement did at the outset serve legitimate security needs, however according to the authors of the report, those restrictions remained in force after the need for security had come to its end, and serve at present for inappropriate purposes.

With all due respect this last statement by the report's authors is by *its very nature groundless.*

As to the general security need that is at the basis of the restrictions on movement imposed in Judea and Samaria, we wish to remind that from the very beginning, that is, since September 2000, the State of Israel has been coping with a terror attack of unprecedented strength, which is addressed towards the citizens of Israel wherever they may be, and towards Israelis who live and pass through the region.

In this matter, please refer for example to the words of the former President of the Israeli Supreme Court, his honorable Justice [Aharon] Barak, regarding the Alfei Menashe affair [dealing with security in the Alfei Menashe settlement] as follows . . .

> In September 2000 the second *intifada* [uprising] broke out. A mighty attack of acts of terrorism landed upon Israel, and upon Israelis in the Judea, Samaria, and Gaza Strip areas (hereinafter—*the area*). Most of the terrorist attacks were directed toward civilians. They struck at men and at women; at elderly and at infant. Entire families lost their loved ones. The attacks were designed to take human life. . . .
>
> Israel took a series of steps to defend the lives of her residents. Military operations were carried out against terrorist organizations. These operations were intended to defeat the Palestinian terrorist infrastructure and prevent a reoccurrence of terrorist acts. . . . These steps did not provide a sufficient answer to the immediate need to halt the severe terrorist attacks. Innocent people continued to pay with life and limb . . ."

*The State of Israel has been coping with a terror attack of unprecedented strength.*

## The Legal Right to Oppose Terror

As the former honorable President of the Israeli Supreme court, Mr. Aharon Barak, has noticed, in the ongoing fight against terrorism, the security forces face various and different threats. In order to provide an answer to the threats addressed towards the State of Israel, and against the Israelis who live in the area, the military commander is authorized, *and is often obligated,* to undertake various security measures that may, as much as possible, provide a response to these threats.

---

*Even though restrictions on movement are imposed, many efforts are made to relieve the local population.*

---

Thus, as part of his duty to protect the State of Israel, and the lives of the area's residents, the military commander undertakes security measures targeted at thwarting terrorist attacks. This authority has also been recognized in the ruling, in the verdict pronounced by the honorable judge (her title at the time), [Dorit] Beinisch, in HCJ 9593/04, *the head of the Yanon village council v. the military commander of the IDF forces in Judea and Samaria,* (2006) (Hereinafter: "*The Yanon Village Affair*"), as follows:

> The Judea and Samaria area is held by the State of Israel under a belligerent occupation, and there is no dispute that the military commander, appointed on behalf of the State of Israel over the region, is authorized to instruct, through an order issued, on the closure of the entire area, or part of it, and by this prevent the entry and exit of people from the closed area. This authority of the military commander derives from the belligerent occupation rules, based on the international public law, the military commander's duties are to assure the peace of the region's residents, their security, and the region's public order. . . .

Unfortunately, the terrorism threat which took the lives of over a thousand Israeli citizens, necessitates in certain cases, that there be a restriction on the freedom of movement within the area. *This need derives from the fact that the Palestinian terrorism operates from within the civil population under its auspices, whilst obstinately and severely violating international law.*

This intricate reality dictates, in certain cases, the imposition of restrictions on movement within the area.

## Care for the Local Population

One has to point out that when imposing these restrictions, the military commander recognizes the local population's needs. As such he undertakes great effort, including the allotment of vast resources, in order to alleviate, to the extent possible, any difficulties caused to that part of the population which is not involved in terrorist activity. He must do all this in parallel with fulfillment of his duty under the international law, to fight terrorism and to secure the public order, and public life in the area.

Thus, even though restrictions on movement are imposed, many efforts are made to relieve the local population, either by verifying the existence of reasonable alternatives for the movement of Palestinians in the area, and also by placing special emphasis on the freedom of movement of ambulances, medical crews, and those residents who are in need of medical care.

Finally, it should be stressed that operating in its jurisdiction as the High Court of Justice, the Israeli Supreme Court has affirmed, in a long list of verdicts, that the military commander is authorized to impose restrictions on movement within the area, in order to provide a solution to legitimate security needs, as long as these restrictions respect the principles of proportionality.

## The Importance of Barriers

One chapter of the report extensively examines the effect of physical obstructions placed by security forces on the roads of Judea and Samaria—i.e., physical blockages, manned barriers, and movable surprise barriers. The report claims that these obstructions dissect Judea and Samaria into segments, and that passage between those segments is limited and controlled.

Contrary to what is claimed in the report, the barriers so placed by security forces on the various roads of Judea and Samaria, have a clear security purpose. They constitute an important aspect of the overall effort by security forces to disrupt the activity of Palestinian terrorist organizations. These barriers aim to render the passage of attackers, and the transfer of war materials within the area, more difficult. The barriers assist in preventing the free and uncontrolled movement of terrorists in the region. Furthermore, where terrorists have attempted to execute attacks, (whether those attacks be within the region itself, or on the Israeli home front), the existence of barricades makes it much harder for the attackers to subsequently escape. . . .

---

*One can say with certainty that the operation of road barriers has in recent years, thwarted dozens—perhaps hundreds, of sabotage attacks aimed at Israeli targets.*

---

This is evidenced by the fact that in recent years, *thousands of terrorist activists have been arrested* at various roadblocks and barriers in Judea and Samaria. Some of those arrested were potential suicide bombers, high-ranking members of terrorist organizations, collaborators and more. In addition the roadblocks have prevented the passage of war materials, *including explosive belts and various weapons*, which were intended for use against specific Israeli targets and innocent civilians.

In actual fact, one can say with certainty that the operation of road barriers has in recent years, thwarted dozens—perhaps hundreds, of sabotage attacks aimed at Israeli targets.

IDF forces [Israel Defense Forces] are well aware of the problems faced by the local population in those parts of Judea and Samaria where roadblocks are in use. In response, they are set to offer appropriate solutions where possible. Some of the solutions adopted by the IDF in recent years include the

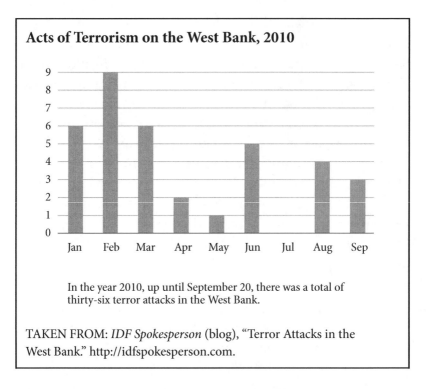

**Acts of Terrorism on the West Bank, 2010**

In the year 2010, up until September 20, there was a total of thirty-six terror attacks in the West Bank.

TAKEN FROM: *IDF Spokesperson* (blog), "Terror Attacks in the West Bank." http://idfspokesperson.com.

implementation of procedures which aim to provide better treatment of the local population, residing in the area and who regularly pass through the barriers situated there, and at the roadblocks between Israel and the area.

In addition, the Ministry of Defence has invested vast resources (many millions), into improvement of the infrastructure of the various checkpoints, in order to relieve the passage of the general population.

## A Proportional Security Measure

The implementation of barriers and roadblocks in Judea and Samaria necessarily causes certain discomfort and delay of movement within the area. Considering, however, the proven security effectiveness of these barriers and roadblocks, and their importance in the overall effort of fighting terrorism, and the steps undertaken in order to alleviate the damage caused to the local population, roadblocks and barriers may be viewed as a much-needed and proportional security measure.

It seems appropriate here to refer to what the former vice-president of the Israeli Supreme Court, Justice Mishael M. Cheshin, has written in a petition that dealt with the issue of roadblocks in the Nablus region:

> We all agree that the situation of the villages' residents is not easy, but we have to take into account at the same time the security considerations, which led to the burdening of the traveling on the roads. As has been explained to us by the State representative, in writing as well as orally, the city of Nablus, serves as the source for terrorists who set out on killing and destruction missions in the territories and in Israel, and all those means undertaken by the IDF, are only for the purpose of protecting the lives of Israeli citizens and settlers in Judea and Samaria. . . .
>
> We have heard the arguments of the petitioners' lawyers, and with all the empathy which we may feel towards the petitioners, since all of them, or at least the majority among them, certainly did not sin—we did not find any cause to tell the respondent that actions committed by him, deviate from the domain of reasonability or from the suitable proportionality. Indeed, the respondent could have also taken other means to protect the lives, but we have not found that the way he undertook indicates any fault or aberration. . . .

## Restrictions and Prohibitions to Movement on the Road

The report refers to roads on which the movement of Palestinians has been limited. It is claimed that there are a large number of roads on which free movement is almost exclusively confined to Israeli citizens in general, and settlers of Judea and Samaria in particular.

Our answer to this argument, is that the *absolute majority* of the roads in Judea and Samaria, enable the movement of

Palestinians, without the need for a certain permit. Only in a *few isolated* cases, where the measure is proportionate, and there is a clear security concern requiring as much, will the military commander limit Palestinian movement on the road.

Take for example, the illustration cited in the report of the 443 road. As stated in the report, the movement of vehicles carrying Palestinian license plates is partially limited on this axis. What has not been mentioned in the report, is that this limitation was imposed by the military commander for lack of any alternative, and as a response to a long list of murderous terrorist events along the road, which have claimed the lives of several Israeli citizens and injured many others who were traveling on the road in question.

---

*Bear in mind that in many cases, security needs required movement restrictions to be imposed on Israeli citizens only.*

---

With complete understanding of the importance of freedom of movement for the local population, the military commander could not consent to the reality of the given security concern, at the beginning of the fighting events, when every Israeli who drove along road no. 443—was putting his/her life at risk.

Bear in mind that in many cases, security needs required movement restrictions to be imposed on Israeli citizens only—a fact which was not mentioned in the report. As an example, we shall point out that travel on all roads in the "A" area, is prohibited for Israelis (unless a specific permit is issued by the authorized entities). Similar prohibitions apply to many other roads which extend throughout the area.

Nonetheless, it is important to note that ongoing assessments of the matters, based on the security reality, are conducted, and as far as possible, . . . alleviations will be carried out in favor of the local population.

# The Fayyad Government Fails to Meet Expectations

*Nathan J. Brown*

*Nathan J. Brown is a professor of political science at George Washington University. In the following viewpoint, he reports that Salam Fayyad, the Palestinian prime minister, failed to live up to expectations. Fayyad did not bring Palestinians to the brink of statehood or build any institutions. Though Brown does not view these as personal failings, the expectations set for Fayyad were far too high.*

As you read, consider the following questions:

1. Who were Salam Fayyad's predecessors?
2. What are some of the things that Brown claims Fayyad "did not do"?
3. What does the author state Fayyad "did do"?

If Palestinian Authority Prime Minister Salam Fayyad's political career came to an end today, he could still proudly claim to be Palestine's most accomplished prime minister ever. The problem is that all of his predecessors—Ahmad Hilmi, Mahmoud Abbas, Ahmed Qurei, and Ismail Haniyya—were impotent, transitory, or frustrated occupants of the post, and collectively set a very low bar. But judged by the enormous expectations and hoopla his Western cheerleaders burdened him with, Fayyad will leave only disappointment behind him.

Nathan J. Brown, "No Savior: The West's Lofty Expectations for Salam Fayyad Went Far Beyond What He Was Ever Able to Deliver," *Foreign Policy*, no. 853, June 17, 2011. Reproduced with permission.

The prime minister's departure from the Palestinian political scene appears likely but not inevitable. With Fatah and Hamas striving to form a unity government, Fayyad may very well be sacrificed on the altar of Palestinian unity.

Neither the sunny nor the cynical view of Fayyad is fair. His optimistic smile obscured an impossible situation: Fayyad's main achievement has not been to build the structures of a Palestinian state, but to stave off the collapse of those structures that did exist. An equally important achievement was his ability to persuade Western observers that he was doing much more. In the process, however, he raised expectations far beyond his ability to deliver.

---

*The state-like political structures now in the West Bank and Gaza were either built during the heyday of the Oslo process in the 1990s or in the more distant days of Jordanian and British rule.*

---

## What Fayyad Did Not Do

In enumerating Fayyad's accomplishments, it is necessary—if churlish—to begin by explaining what Fayyad did not accomplish.

First, he did not build any institutions. The state-like political structures now in the West Bank and Gaza were either built during the heyday of the Oslo process in the 1990s or in the more distant days of Jordanian and British rule.

Second, he did not bring Palestinians to the brink of statehood. The Palestinian Authority, for all its problems, was actually far more ready for statehood on the eve of the Second Intifada in 1999 than it is on the possible eve of the third in 2011. A dozen years ago, Palestine had full security control of its cities, a set of institutions that united the West Bank and Gaza, a flourishing civil society, and a set of legitimate structures for writing authoritative laws and implementing them.

Those accomplishments were in retreat long before Fayyad took office, and he was hardly able to restore them.

Third, Fayyad did not strengthen the rule of law. He could not have done so, since the only legitimate law-making body the Palestinians have, the Legislative Council, has not met since he came to power.

---

*He led half of a dysfunctional Palestinian Authority, governed scattered bits of territory in the West Bank, and was forced to rattle the cup constantly in order to pay the bills.*

---

Fourth, Fayyad did not prove to Palestinians that they should rely on themselves. Just the opposite. He showed Palestinians that if they relied on him, foreigners would show them the money. At the heady days at the beginning of Oslo, the United States pledged half a billion dollars for the entire five-year process during which the parties were supposed to negotiate a permanent agreement. They have given Fayyad more than that almost every year that he has been in office. The Europeans have opened the purse strings for him too. It is utterly baffling that a figure so completely dependent on Western diplomatic and financial support would be seen by outsiders as an icon of Palestinian self-help.

Finally, he did not bring economic development to the West Bank. What he made possible was a real but unsustainable recovery based on aid and relaxation of travel restrictions. Year-to-year economic indicators in both the West Bank and Gaza are dependent on foreign assistance, and even more on the political and security situation. Fayyad can thus take some credit for the upturn, but Hamas can make a similar claim for the mild improvements in Gaza since Israel relaxed some of the closure last year [2010]. Neither has laid the groundwork for real development or attraction of foreign investment. Nor could they in the stultifying and uncertain political environment.

None of these failings was personal. Fayyad could not have accomplished any of these goals even had he wanted to. He led half of a dysfunctional Palestinian Authority, governed scattered bits of territory in the West Bank, and was forced to rattle the cup constantly in order to pay the bills.

## What Fayyad Did Do

However, if Fayyad could not walk on water, he did an almost miraculous job of not drowning. This is not to damn Fayyad with faint praise; the prime minister assumed control of a Palestinian Authority that was unable to pay all of its salaries, deeply mistrusted by Israel, and treated as irrelevant by many Palestinians.

His first and most impressive accomplishment was to gain the trust of Western governments. The unrealistic hopes placed in his premiership were partly a testimony to the esteem in which he was held in some international circles. Secretary of State Hillary Clinton has spoken of her pride in his efforts and informed Palestinian youth that Fayyad has given them hope. No diplomatic statement from Western governments is complete without a kind word for his accomplishments. Fayyad was even able to earn a grudging Israeli trust through renewed security cooperation and efforts to rebuild the Palestinian security services. These accomplishments allowed him to pay government salaries, redeploy police, and attract enormous amounts of aid.

And Fayyad was able to win some modest victories in Palestinian governance. The security services became less partisan, public finances became more transparent (even without any domestic oversight), corruption likely decreased, pockets of the civil service were rebuilt on a more professional basis, and basic order in Palestinian cities was improved. When it comes to progress in these areas—sharply limited but still significant—Fayyad can even claim to have gone beyond maintenance to improving the Palestinian situation beyond where it stood in 1999.

## Fatah vs. Hamas

The divisions between the two main Palestinian political factions, Fatah and Hamas, are not religious—as nearly all Palestinian Muslims are from the Sunni branch of Islam—but rather ideological differences in objectives, governance, and relations with Israel. Tensions between Fatah and Hamas began to rise in 2005 after the death of the charismatic leader Yasser Arafat. After Hamas's parliamentary election victory in January 2006, relations were marked by sporadic factional fighting and several assassinations of both Hamas and Fatah leaders. The conflict grew more intense after the two parties repeatedly failed to reach a deal to share government power, escalating in June 2007 into an outright civil war. As of August 2007, the Palestinian Territories are split into a Hamas-controlled Gaza Strip and a Fatah-dominated West Bank.

*Wide Angle, "Gaza E.R.: Fatah vs. Hamas,"*
*August 14, 2007. www.pbs.org.*

## The Poverty of Politics

All along, however, this was a difficult juggling act. Enthusiastic international support would continue only so long as it was possible to pretend that Fayyad was making dramatic gains; domestic acceptance of Fayyad was dependent on his continuing to pay salaries and provide for basic order. Pulling aside the curtain and revealing that Palestinians were not building a state thus risked undermining Western support for him, which would in turn remove the raison d'être of his premiership in Palestinian eyes.

Thus Fayyadism was a political house of cards. There was no domestic foundation for Fayyad's efforts; for Palestinians, he was simply an unsolicited gift from the United States and Europe—a welcome one for some, but not for others. And to his international backers, Fayyad was completely frank about his limitations: His efforts, he said, would only pay off in the context of a meaningful diplomatic process that reinforced the drive toward statehood. This was an ingredient that has been missing for many years, and Fayyad was powerless to procure it.

Earlier this year, there were signs that Fayyad himself had begun to look for ways to escape Fayyadism. It was Fayyad, rather than Fatah and Palestinian President Mahmoud Abbas, who reached out to Hamas in February. The reconciliation file was quickly snatched out of his hands, however, and his hold on the premiership is now on the bargaining table.

What is remarkable, however, is how Fayyadism soldiered on in some Western eyes even after Fayyad himself had begun to distance himself from it. American pundits continued to trumpet his successes without missing a beat right up until the April reconciliation agreement. In March, Thomas Friedman was still writing about Fayyad's gaining momentum and even upped the ante by claiming that his program posed the "biggest threat to Iran's strategy." Meanwhile top policy makers continued to be mesmerized by Fayyad's poll numbers, which were less bad than those of most other leaders, and simply ignored the hollowness at the core of their own policies. Nor did the polls translate into any kind of political party or movement that could have run in, much less won, an election—if one were ever held.

## The Perils of Positive Thinking

For years, Fayyad's soft talk and cheery dedication enabled policy makers throughout the world to ignore the brewing crisis. And this may be where Fayyad, despite his impressive management skills, did Palestinians a disservice.

In 2009, the incoming [Barack] Obama administration was quickly lured into a set of approaches (many inherited from the [George W.] Bush years) that proved their complete bankruptcy this year—ignoring Gaza and allowing its population to be squeezed hard, pretending that there was a meaningful Israeli-Palestinian negotiation process at hand, assuming that Hamas could be dealt with after the peace process and Fayyad had worked their magic, and making the paradoxical and erroneous assumption that the best way to build Palestinian institutions was to rely on a specific, virtuous individual.

Fayyad cannot be held primarily responsible for this collective self-delusion; at most, he facilitated it. And in the process he provided all actors with a breathing space that is now disappearing. Ultimately, the ones who convinced themselves he was capable of completely transforming Palestine are most responsible for squandering the brief respite his premiership offered.

# The Fayyad Government Has a Serious Plan for Peace

### Ali Jarbawi

*Ali Jarbawi is the minister of planning and administrative development in the Palestinian government of Prime Minister Salam Fayyad. In the following viewpoint, he argues that the Fayyad plan for the nonviolent, timely construction of a state of Palestine is workable. He says the plan demonstrates that Palestinians are committed to peace. It is Israel, he says, that is unwilling to negotiate because Israel wants to expand settlements and retain the occupation. Jarbawi concludes that the Palestinian vision of a two-state solution is in line with that of the international community.*

As you read, consider the following questions:

1. What does Jarbawi say is the time frame for the establishment of a Palestinian state through the Fayyad plan?

2. What does the Israeli experience to date encourage Israelis to believe, according to Jarbawi?

3. Why does Jarbawi say that international political intervention and financial support are necessary to resolve the Palestinian-Israeli conflict?

The program of the current Palestinian government is commonly referred to as the Fayyad Plan, for Premier Salam Fayyad. It calls for all Palestinian institutions, and Palestinian society as a whole, to unite behind a state-building effort. The program embodies an authentically Palestinian initiative to work proactively and constructively toward establishing the state of Palestine through nonviolent means over a two-year time frame, despite the lack of progress in negotiations and continued military occupation.

## A Partner for Peace

The Fayyad Plan, specifically its ongoing implementation, demonstrates that there is a positive and engaged partner on the Palestinian side who is committed to a two-state solution with Israel. The stark contrast with Israeli decisions to further expand settlements beyond the "green line" [based on the 1949 Armistice Agreements] is beginning to unmask Israel as an unwilling negotiating partner.

The program provides a path to independence and sovereignty that can be pursued irrespective of the status and progress of the negotiating track. In specifying a two-year time horizon, however, the program has been viewed by some observers as controversial and ambitious. Yet, after 17 years of negotiations, the formulation of new approaches to realizing the two-state solution by the Palestinian Authority (PA) has been long overdue.

> *The Fayyad Plan . . . demonstrates that there is a positive and engaged partner on the Palestinian side who is committed to a two-state solution with Israel.*

Furthermore, the World Bank reported in September 2009 that the PA was "well-positioned for the establishment of a Palestinian state at any point in the near future," noting that "relative to other countries in the region, the public sector in the West Bank and Gaza is arguably already more effective and efficient."

The PA has quite clearly demonstrated its determination to deliver on commitments made in the program. There is a serious, ongoing effort, backed by the international community, to complete the establishment of efficient and effective Palestinian state institutions. This is bearing fruit in the West Bank and, if the embargo is lifted, can be replicated in the Gaza Strip as well. The program is designed to deliver tangible results in spite of the perverse system of geographical demarcations, checkpoints and other movement restrictions that have no place in a modern democratic state.

The overall objective of the Fayyad Plan is therefore to realize, through peaceful means, the Palestinian vision of ending the Israeli occupation and establishing an independent sovereign state on the 1967 borders. This is in the Palestinian national interest and is in lockstep with the international consensus. At the same time, the PA has not turned its back on negotiations. All we are asking for is that the negotiations be credible and that they be focused on the final-status issues and subject to a time limit.

## Israel Is Not a Credible Partner

There is no doubt that Israel, on the other hand, has significant political and economic incentives to postpone a resolution of the conflict. The settlement enterprise, launched and nurtured by the Israeli government, has yielded substantial gains of land and other natural resources. It has also curried favor with political factions that remain wedded to the vision of "Greater Israel" and Israeli sovereignty over both East and West Jerusalem. In this light, it is not surprising that Israel is satisfied with the status quo of open-ended negotiations. Their experience to date encourages Israelis to believe that, with the passage of time, the oppression and suppression they can apply as occupier will reliably elicit acts of violent resistance, reinforcing their stock argument that the Palestinians are not a credible partner for peacemaking.

The fact that the Palestinian program has found such favor with the international community, and that the two-year time frame has gained currency and momentum in international political circles, is a major challenge to this status quo. In effect, from the Israeli perspective, the program has poked a stick in the ever-turning wheel of the negotiating process. Israel is now having a hard time casting the PA in the role of "unwilling partner" and is in serious danger of being cast in that role itself.

---

*There is no doubt that Israel . . . has significant political and economic incentives to postpone a resolution of the conflict.*

---

Israel also fears that time may no longer be on its side as the international community begins to realize what Palestinians have known for years, namely that a resolution of the conflict between the two parties, one of which enjoys overwhelming security and economic power relative to the other, is not possible without international political intervention as well as financial support.

The ongoing implementation of the Palestinian government program represents, for the first time in years, visible and tangible progress toward making the two-state solution a reality. This is proving that we Palestinians are a real and engaged partner and are moving forward positively toward realizing a vision shared with the international community. This program is a historic opportunity to resolve the conflict that must not be missed.

# Periodical and Internet Sources Bibliography

*The following articles have been selected to supplement the diverse views presented in this chapter.*

| | |
|---|---|
| Gwen Ackerman and Calev Ben-David | "Israel Approves New Construction in West Bank Settlements," *Bloomberg Businessweek*, March 13, 2011. |
| B'Tselem | "By Hook and by Crook: Israeli Settlement Policy in the West Bank," July 2010. www .btselem.org. |
| IRIN | "ISRAEL-OPT: West Bank Movement Restrictions Can Be Lethal for Palestinians, Says Amnesty Report," June 4, 2007. www.irinnews.org. |
| *Israel Matzav* (blog) | "Should We Laugh or Cry at Salam Fayyad?," February 3, 2011. http://israelmatzav .blogspot.com. |
| Yaakov Katz and Tovah Lazaroff | "'Fayyad Is Inciting Violence,'" *Jerusalem Post*, March 1, 2010. |
| Karin Laub | "Israel to Ease West Bank Movement Restrictions," *Huffington Post*, May 24, 2010. www .huffingtonpost.com. |
| Stephen Lendman | "Denying Palestinians Free Movement in the West Bank," Global Research, May 1, 2008. www.globalresearch.ca. |
| David M. Phillips | "The Illegal-Settlements Myth," *Commentary*, December 2009. |
| David Rosenberg | "Fayyad Says Palestinian Institutions Ready for Statehood," *Jerusalem Post*, April 5, 2011. |
| Ari Shavit | "West Bank Settlements Are Israel's Nuclear Meltdown," *Haaretz*, March 17, 2011. |

GLOBALVIEWPOINTS

CHAPTER 4

# International Involvement in the Arab-Israeli Conflict

# The European Union Should Delink the Peace Process from Other Regional Challenges

## Emanuele Ottolenghi

*Emanuele Ottolenghi is executive director of the Transatlantic Institute in Brussels. In the following viewpoint, he notes that the European Union (EU) has close ties with both Israel and Palestine. He notes, however, that Israel generally views Europe as more sympathetic to the Palestinian cause and that Europe does, in fact, expect more concessions from Israel than from the Palestinians. Ottolenghi argues that Europe should be more sympathetic to Israel's security concerns and viewpoint. He concludes that Europe should delink the Palestinian peace process from other regional issues.*

As you read, consider the following questions:

1. What does Ottolenghi say is at the heart of the Arab/ Israeli conflict for Israel?

2. According to Ottolenghi, what is the EU's official position on a final territorial settlement to the Arab-Israeli conflict?

3. What was the EU's position on Israel's security barrier, according to Ottolenghi?

Emanuele Ottolenghi, *Squaring the Circle?: EU-Israel Relations and the Peace Process in the Middle East*, CES—Center for European Studies, January 2010, pp. 5–7, 27–35. Copyright © 2010 by the Center for European Studies. All rights reserved. Reproduced with permission.

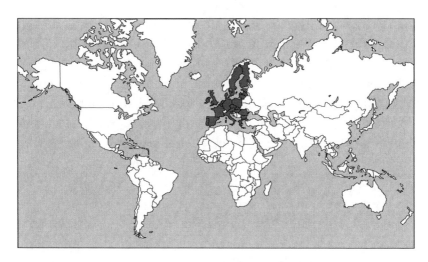

History binds Europe and Israel—centuries of Jewish life in Europe characterised by both bright lights and dark shadows offer a profound and meaningful background to the relation. Europe views the Middle East as a strategic region. Economic interests are also paramount. The EU [European Union] is Israel's largest trading partner. And Israel is the most active participant in the European Neighbourhood Policy [ENP]. Relations are good and the potential for deeper relations is strong. Since signing their first Cooperation Agreement in 1975, Israel and the EU have enjoyed a fruitful bilateral relation which has grown over the years. In 1995, Israel and the EU signed an Association Agreement, which came into force in 2000. Their Action Plan was signed in 2005. An array of additional agreements in disparate fields ensures that Israel and the EU are bound to one another in an ever closer and more intimate embrace.

## The EU, Israel, and Palestine

The EU has also developed an institutional framework for relations with the Palestinian Authority [PA], following the 1993 Oslo Accords between Israel and the PLO [Palestine Liberation Organization]. While the EU-Palestinian partnership is one driven less by economic interest, the political implications of this relation are significant and predate Oslo and the inclusion of the Palestinian Authority into the Barcelona Process and, later, the European Neighbourhood Policy. Ever since the Venice Declaration (1980), Europe has sought an active role in fostering a peace agreement between Israel and the Palestinians. Its financial commitments to and political dialogue with the Palestinian side well predate the opening of a US-PLO dialogue in December 1988. The PLO was allowed to open representative offices in many European countries throughout the late 1970s and 1980s, which in some cases were granted quasi-embassy status. In some cases, EU member states have even granted financial aid to the PLO to run their representative offices. This was not without negative consequences for EU-Israel relations: Europe's political view of the conflict, particularly its willingness to treat the PLO as a legitimate interlocutor well before the PLO renounced terrorism and political violence, cemented Israel's suspicion about a prominent European role in the Middle East peace process.

---

*Europe has managed to become the main financial backer of a fledgling Palestinian Authority while at the same time pursuing a fruitful economic relation with Israel.*

---

This perception, though still a relevant factor, has not impeded a gradual deepening of relations between the EU and the Middle East actors, especially after the 1993 Oslo agreements, which enabled international actors like the EU to seek more active engagement with both sides as a tool to facilitate peace and stability. And whatever the merits of Israel's view on Europe's stance vis-à-vis the Palestine question and ways to bring the Middle East conflict to a peaceful resolution, Europe has managed to become the main financial backer of a fledgling Palestinian Authority while at the same time pursuing a fruitful economic relation with Israel.

# Bridging the Gap

However, a shadow is cast on the ability of Israel and Europe to come closer politically—substantial differences divide them on thorny political themes, ranging from the impact of the Israel-Palestinian conflict on regional stability, the contours of its comprehensive settlement, the broader policy challenges for regional security, to, most importantly, European attempts to increase its influence in the region. Similarly, Europe's growing financial commitment to a Palestinian Authority that, 16 years after the Oslo Accords, remains deeply dependent on external aid raises questions about Europe's ability to make a difference, politically, in the Middle East conflict, even as the bill it is prepared to foot is steadily growing.

What can Europe and Israel do to bridge the political gap that divides them and that significantly affects their otherwise fruitful cooperation? What should be the nature of their bilateral relation? What can be expected of each side? Can bilateral relations be upgraded at the political level? If so, should progress on resolving the Palestinian-Israeli dispute be a precondition for an enhanced political dialogue? Or should the two elements be disjointed? Should the political distance in critical aspects of policy be allowed to stand in the way of closer political cooperation? Should Europe's present financial largesse to the Palestinian Authority be reassessed? Should conditionality be applied, similarly, to Europe's relations with the Palestinians? How is Europe to calibrate its financial aid and political support, especially after the Palestinian body politic split into two seemingly irreconcilable and geographically separated entities, one in the West Bank under the more secular Fatah leadership of President Mahmoud Abbas, and the other in Gaza under the Islamist regime of Hamas? And how can these two bilateral tracks be reconciled in a coherent framework (and should they be)? . . .

## An Intractable Dispute

Simplistic as it may sound, the divergence in views between Israel and the EU on the Israeli-Palestinian dispute is as follows.

For Europe, the conflict is both the cause of other regional problems and the impediment to their solution. Solutions exist, but are elusive due to the recalcitrance of the partners involved. Israel shares much of the burden of blame for failure because, as the stronger party, it must concede more. The elusive peace, ironically, has well-known contours and defined terms—and if achieved, it would set the stage for a new era in the region, where old boundaries and ancient animosities would give way to cooperation, open borders and prosperity.

---

*In the words of Palestinian analyst Ahmed [Al-]Khalidi, "there are no conceivable circumstances in which any Palestinian can concede their own history in favour of the Zionist narrative."*

---

For Israel, at the heart of the conflict lies the inability and unwillingness of the Arab world to recognise the legitimacy of a Jewish state in portions of what Arabs call historic Palestine and for Israelis is the biblical land of Israel. The nature of the conflict does not lend itself to an easy solution—because its existential nature derives from the fact that it is a clash between mutually exclusive national claims that are closely intertwined and rendered more intractable by a religious dimension. Since Oslo's failure, there is a growing consensus among Israelis of all political persuasions that there never was—and perhaps therefore there will never be—a reliable Palestinian partner who would concede that Israel has a legitimate claim which must be reconciled with Palestinian aspirations.

For the Palestinians, Israel's creation was an illegitimate act. This view is prevalent even among those within the Palestinian political and intellectual elites who support a peaceful compromise with Israel. In the words of Palestinian analyst Ahmed [Al-]Khalidi, "there are no conceivable circumstances in which any Palestinian can concede their own history in favour of the Zionist narrative." A two-state solution, even if achieved, would thus hardly put Palestinian irredentist claims to rest.

This leaves the conflict as a proverbial circle that is impossible to square.

Given the gulf that divides them, one would expect Israel and Europe to be constantly at loggerheads over the MEPP [Middle East Peace Process]. And given European insistence on conditionality on the one hand, and Israeli suspicion of European involvement on the other, one would equally presume that progress in the bilateral relation would be hampered by the lack of progress on the diplomatic track.

Yet, in recent years, the EU has taken, and Israel has welcomed, an increasingly active role in promoting a negotiated settlement, as a member of the Quartet [the United States, United Nations (UN), EU, and Russia joined together as a group in mediating the Middle East Peace Process], through its common foreign policy, and by actions of its member states. The [European] Commission has a representative office in Tel Aviv and the Directorate General for Humanitarian Aid of the Commission has an office in Jerusalem. The EU has undertaken a security mission (EUBAM) to monitor the Gaza-Egypt border crossing of Rafah following Israel's disengagement from Gaza in the summer of 2005. And troops from several member states (including Belgium, France, Italy and Spain) constitute the bulk of the beefed up UNIFIL [United Nations Interim Force in Lebanon] force deployed in Lebanon following the July 2006 war between Israel and Hezbollah [a Lebanon-based Islamic militant group]. Germany has provided naval units to patrol off the coast of Lebanon in the framework of a UN-brokered cease-fire under UN Security Council Resolution 1701 and has played an important mediating role on delicate dossiers such as indirect negotiations between Israel and Hezbollah on the return of IDF [Israel Defense Forces] soldiers' remains to Israel.

## Constructive Involvement

Much of this involvement is constructive—though it has not always been the same. It offers Europe a stronger claim to have a say—and a role—in helping the parties shape the final outcome of their negotiations. Regardless, Israel has traditionally viewed Europe's position as more tilted toward the Palestinians, and recent improvements in relations have only partially removed Israeli scepticism at European involvement. This scepticism would be given a new lease of life if the EU chose to break the international isolation of Hamas, the Palestinian branch of the Muslim Brotherhood and a member of the EU terror list, which today rules over Gaza and may keep prominence as a key player in Palestinian politics for the foreseeable future.

Thus, it is important to briefly review Europe's position on the conflict and highlight problematic areas. Europe officially supports a two-state solution, a negotiated settlement where final status issues must be agreed upon by the parties, and a framework that guarantees Israel's security while ensuring the establishment of a viable and democratic Palestinian state.

Despite the fact that, broadly speaking, these remain also Israel's goals, the gulf between the EU and Israel over the peace process is broad. Differences pertain to a number of issues which are central to the final status issues and the outcome of negotiations—namely, borders, settlements, Jerusalem and refugees.

The EU's official position is that a final territorial settlement must take the 1949 provisional armistice lines—the so-called Green Line—as the international boundary, whereby only minor modifications would occur and then only by mu-

# The European Union, Peace, and Hamas

Although the EU [European Union] still only has a supporting role [in the peace process], it can make a tangible contribution in the international peace effort. The EU has long been committed to ending the Israeli-Palestinian conflict, because of its sense of historical responsibility; its geographical proximity to this destabilising conflict; and its growing ambitions to be a global player. Through the European Neighbourhood Policy, the EU has extensive bilateral ties with both Israel and the Palestinian territories. The EU is also the leading donor to the Palestinians, and has been involved on the ground through its efforts in Palestinian nation building and training Palestinian security forces. The EU has even provided a border monitoring mission on the Egypt-Gaza border and it has fought hard to get a seat at the table in diplomatic efforts to support the peace process.

Most importantly, the EU can act as the 'other' voice which makes the idea of engaging Hamas more acceptable to Israel and the US. Until now, Israel, the US, the Europeans and most other countries have tried to isolate Hamas, in the hope of bringing about its collapse. But despite two years of harsh sanctions on the group, Hamas is still in control of Gaza and undermining the peace effort with its attacks on Israel. As long as Hamas remains a leading political and military force on the Palestinian side, its involvement will be needed to curb the violence, stabilise the situation on the ground and, in the longer term, to secure a lasting basis for peace. Hamas' current violent tactics and intemperate rhetoric are unacceptable. But within a favourable environment the organisation may yet transform itself into a more responsible political player.

*Clara Marina O'Donnell,* The EU, Israel and Hamas, *Centre for European Reform, 2008. www.cer.org.uk.*

tual agreement. Similarly, the EU is of the view that settlements are illegal under international law, and therefore the terms of negotiations are only about the time line for Israel's removal of settlements, not about whether some such communities should remain under Israeli sovereignty. Finally, the EU does not explicitly express a commitment to Jerusalem being re-divided into two—an Israeli West Jerusalem and a Palestinian East Jerusalem. Instead, it is committed to a 'fair solution' of the Jerusalem issue. However, by considering any Israeli construction in East Jerusalem to be an extension of its settlement policy and by supporting Palestinian institution building in East Jerusalem, in practice the EU takes a position close to the Palestinian one.

---

*Israel has traditionally viewed Europe's position as more titled toward the Palestinians, and recent improvements in relations have only partially removed Israeli scepticism at European involvement.*

---

On refugees, the EU position refers to similarly vague language. However, it is hard to claim that Europe is impartial—especially when one considers its reluctance to recognise Israel's right to exist *as a Jewish state*. The EU official position is that taking sides on a matter that is the subject of negotiations would be detrimental to a successful political negotiation. In fact, Europe has already sided against Israel and with the Palestinian position on settlements, borders and Jerusalem—by siding with Israel on its nature and character as a nation-state it would make a positive contribution to the peace process, not the contrary.

## The Barrier and the US-Israel Understanding

Two episodes illustrate best this incomprehension in recent times—Europe's position with regard to Israel's decision to build a security barrier along much of the West Bank, especially in relation to the July 2004 International Court of Justice's advisory opinion on the matter; and Europe's reaction to US-Israel understandings about settlements and borders, which then US President George W. Bush and then Israeli Prime Minister Ariel Sharon reached in April 2004.

On the barrier, Europe essentially made two assumptions, based on which it voted at the UN to support the International Court of Justice advisory opinion against Israel's barrier. The first assumption is that Israel can only defend itself by means of an international law that, because it lacks adequate instruments to deal with asymmetric conflict such as the case of terrorism, leaves Israel unable to defend its citizens. The barrier, just like targeted killings, is judged according to abstract principles of international law that fail to acknowledge the nature of terrorism and the imperatives of a sovereign state to protect its civilians from wanton aggression. The second assumption is that, despite all evidence to the contrary, at any rate the barrier is neither effective nor justified. It is not effective because it is through political dialogue, rather than military action and preventive measures, that terrorism will be neutralised. And it is not justified because it inflicts undue suffering and hardships to the Palestinian civilian population.

---

*For Europe, peace is not just imperative but also possible—and a by-product of mainly Israeli concessions.*

---

On the US-Israel understanding, Europe again seems to take the view that on the issue of borders, negotiations have nothing to do with boundary demarcation, but only with terms of Israeli withdrawal to a pre-established line. It is worth recalling that the American-Israeli quid pro quo of April 2004, entailed an Israeli promise to evacuate the Gaza Strip and part of the northern West Bank in exchange for a generic commitment by the US to defend Israel's territorial claims over large settlement blocs and against Palestinian demands for a right of return in future negotiations. Despite the fact that both guarantees are recognised as the necessary concessions Palestinians will have to make if there ever will be a peace agreement, the EU found it improvident that America had stated the obvious in its guarantees to Sharon.

Conditionality—the European position according to which progress in political relations is conditional upon progress on the peace track—is the direct result of this difference. For Europe, peace is not just imperative but also possible—and a by-product of mainly Israeli concessions. This view does not sufficiently take into account the broader regional context and its own dynamics, which are independent of the conflict, though they may affect it. Enduring memories, historically rooted grievances and religiously driven identities have been the cause of continued hostilities throughout the history of the Arab-Israeli conflict and cannot be discounted or overcome merely through a set of Israeli concessions.

## Policy Recommendations

Given the closeness of bilateral relations and yet the distance that separates Israel and the EU over peacemaking, what can the EU do to best serve its interest and improve its relations with Israel?

- The EU should rebalance its priorities in the Middle East, and rate developments in other fields at least as high as progress in the peace process. It should recognise that other regional problems (e.g., the Iranian nuclear programme) actually impede progress between Israel and the Palestinians.

- Decoupling the conflict from other regional challenges does not mean relegating the MEPP to a secondary role; it means refusing to let vital European interests become hostage to progress on the peace track; it also means demanding that Arab regimes stop using the Arab-Israeli conflict as a pretext for lack of internal change and it means recognising that some regional challenges exist quite independently of Israel's existence and lack of Palestinian independence.

- The EU should therefore consider decoupling progress on the MEPP from the upgrade of political ties with Israel. Clearly, there is much to be gained in an ever closer relation between the two sides—and Israel's experience in such disparate fields as homeland security and renewable energy technologies makes a closer cooperation highly desirable. An upgraded political relation would strengthen, not weaken, Europe's ability to influence Israeli thinking and acting on the MEPP and it could foster progress rather than hampering it.

- The EU should add a pronouncement on final status issues about Israel's nature as a nation-state of the Jewish people alongside its already stated support for the type of territorial arrangements a final status agreement would entail; such a statement would strengthen the already existing understanding between Israel and the US on the inapplicability of Palestinian demands on the refugee issue and would give a strong signal to Israeli leaders that concessions will not be expected at the price of Israel's ultimate survival.

- The EU should improve its monitoring and review mechanisms on funding for NGO [nongovernmental organization] projects through its various existing mechanisms—including the EU's Partnership for Peace and the European Instrument for Democracy and Human Rights—ensuring that its funds are not used for purposes that are contrary to its stated policies and values.

- The EU should carefully review its approach to other countries that benefit from access to and participation in the ENP so as not to strengthen the impression that it applies a double standard against Israel.

*The EU should rebalance its priorities in the Middle East and rate developments in other fields at least as high as progress in the peace process.*

On the Palestinian side, the EU should consider adopting these new measures:

- If conditionality is to remain the yardstick of its relation with Israel, the EU should make delivery of EU financial assistance conditional on Palestinian political change as well as in areas that are critical to the advancement of the peace agenda—including education and media;

- The EU should not drop its adherence to Quartet principles of negotiations with the Palestinian government;

- The EU should be more discerning in the kind of Palestinian NGO projects it supports and should devote more funds to civil society projects inside the PA administered territories.

# France and the United States Have Moved Closer on the Arab-Israeli Conflict

## Justin Vaïsse

*Justin Vaïsse is a French historian and a senior fellow in foreign policy at the Brookings Institution. In the following viewpoint, he argues that French and American approaches to the Middle East peace process have converged in recent years. Both France and the United States want an end to Palestinian terrorism and a two-state solution. Vaïsse notes that differences remain; for example, the United States tends to lump Palestinian terrorism in with al Qaeda, while the French believe that Hamas must be seen as a potential negotiating partner. Still, overall, he concludes, France and America are working together for peace in the Middle East.*

As you read, consider the following questions:

1. According to Vaïsse, what did the Bush administration see as a more crucial regional issue than the peace process in the Middle East?

2. How did France's response to the war in Lebanon in 2006 differ from the US response, according to Vaïsse?

3. Does Vaïsse believe that Sarkozy has radically changed France's stance toward the Middle East? Why or why not?

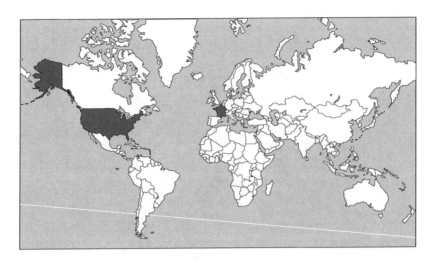

It would be an understatement to say that France and the United States have not always seen eye to eye with each other on the Arab-Israeli conflict. Indeed, this issue has caused some of the most vitriolic diplomatic disputes between Paris and Washington [DC] of the last decades, especially in the 1970s.

## Greater Agreement

More recently, however, the scope of disagreement has tended to narrow, and has given way to increased understanding and cooperation. This was certainly the case during the Oslo peace process years (1993–2000), this was largely the case during the first few months of the road map [for peace] initiative undertaken by the Quartet [a group formed by the United Nations (UN), United States (US), European Union (EU), and Russia to facilitate peace negotiations] (2003), and this has also been the case in the recent months, with the efforts led by Secretary of State Condoleezza Rice to revive the dialogue between the two parties. As a symbol of this convergence, French Foreign Minister Bernard Kouchner recently offered to host a donors' conference in Paris to complement the peace conference scheduled to take place in Annapolis later this month [November 2007].

Does this mean that France and the US are now in complete agreement on this issue? Does the replacement of President Jacques Chirac by Nicolas Sarkozy—who did not hesitate to trumpet his friendship not only for the US, but for Israel as well, during the presidential campaign—usher in a new era of agreement on the Arab-Israeli conflict? If there are reasons to be optimistic, expectations should not get out of hand, as divergences in analysis and interests remain, and the situation on the ground is, in any case, both messy and worrying. Before getting to the specifics of agreements and disagreements between France and the United States, it is useful to review the events of the past few years from a Franco-American perspective.

*The scope of disagreement has tended to narrow, and has given way to increased understanding and cooperation.*

## From the Peace Process to the Road Map

The "hands-off" approach adopted by the [George W.] Bush administration toward the Israeli-Palestinian conflict—a strong contrast with the policy of its predecessor—was a cause of great concern in Paris. In spite of the short-lived hope generated by the road map, French-US perceptions of the Middle East have been marked by divergence, on three issues at least.

First, the primacy of the Israeli-Palestinian peace process for the whole region, a strongly held view in Paris, was disputed by the Bush administration. Many inside this administration considered other regional problems as more critical—especially, it soon turned out, the lack of freedom and democracy, most notably in Iraq. "The road to Jerusalem goes through Baghdad," rather than the reverse French view, was the slogan encapsulating this argument in 2002–2003, with the hope that regime change in Iraq would "serve as a dramatic and inspiring example of freedom for other nations in the region," including the Palestinians, in the words of President Bush in February 2003.

The second issue was the conceptual link established by the Bush administration between al Qaeda [the terrorist group responsible for the September 11, 2001, terrorist attacks on the United States] and Palestinian terrorist groups, in the context of a "global war on terror" in which the US, Israel, and the rest of the civilized world faced . . . a single, monolithic enemy. Seen from Paris, if terrorism from any source is always to be strongly condemned, this view was analytically wrong and politically damaging. In contrast to al Qaeda, with which it is not possible to negotiate anything, Palestinians have legitimate political objectives, and the strategy should be to dissociate the terrorists or armed branch from the moderates or political branch—with which a settlement will ultimately be found. By lumping al Qaeda and Palestinians together, the "global war on terror" de-legitimizes Palestinian claims and ultimately plays into the hands of the radicals.

The third issue is closely related to the second, and has to do with the strength of the Palestinian leadership. Paris had supported [Palestinian leader] Yasser Arafat in the past, certainly not because he was a flawless leader, but out of conviction that lasting peace could only be achieved through direct talks between the two enemies recognizing each other's existence and legitimacy. Ariel Sharon's siege of Arafat's Ramallah headquarters in 2001–2002, George W. Bush's prerequisite that Yasser Arafat goes away before anything happens, the lack of support for Mahmoud Abbas when he succeeded Arafat, the unilateral nature of Sharon's withdrawal from Gaza, the insistence that Palestinians hold free and fair elections in January 2006 but the refusal to accept the consequences of their outcome [when radical Islamic group Hamas won]: all these decisions gave the impression that Israel, the United States and, sometimes, the international community, were ready to take

Palestinians seriously only if they underwent radical change to their liking. The problem is that in order to have a peace process, you need a moderate, solid and legitimate Palestinian leadership to negotiate with—but in order to get this kind of leadership, you need a peace process.

---

*By lumping al Qaeda and Palestinians together, the "global war on terror" de-legitimizes Palestinian claims and ultimately plays into the hands of the radicals.*

---

## The Barrier and Other Issues

Since 2001, many episodes have illustrated these differences in views.

The building of the West Bank barrier, while justifiable on security grounds, was criticized by Paris and the international community, and to a much lesser extent by the US, in as much as it did not go along the Green Line (the 1949 Armistice line) but cut into the West Bank, and reduced Palestinians' ability to move around, work or cultivate their fields, thereby radicalizing many.

While George W. Bush accepted Sharon's unilateral disengagement plan from Gaza in 2004–2005, Paris and the EU as a whole were ambivalent at first, not only as a matter of principle (peace cannot be achieved unilaterally, and priority should be given to the road map), but also out of concern that this could impede the peace process for many years and lead to an acceleration of construction of settlements in the West Bank, as comments by Dov Weisglass, a senior aide to Sharon—and subsequent developments since 2005—have seemed to confirm. However, France and the EU, inside the Quartet, gradually warmed up to the idea and supported it, provided this would be a first step towards a more permanent settlement of the Israeli-Palestinian conflict.

Reaction to Hamas victory in January 2006 was as firm in Paris as it was in Washington. The Quartet asked the new government to recognize Israel as one of the preconditions for continuing development aid. Paris, however, while considering Hamas to be a terrorist organization, holds that it can change in the future—as the PLO [Palestine Liberation Organization] did in 1989—and possibly become, once it has recognized Israel and renounced terrorism, a party to negotiate with, while—despite statements to the contrary—Washington acts as if it did not consider this possible.

When the war in Lebanon broke out in July 2006, Washington expressed its tacit support, hoping that Hezbollah [the militant Lebanese Islamic group] would be significantly weakened. Paris was more doubtful on this point, and feared that a disproportionate reaction would have terrible effects on the population of Lebanon as a whole. To take the Israeli concern into account, Paris and other European capitals took the lead in reinforcing the UNIFIL [United Nations Interim Force in Lebanon] to better act as a buffer force in Southern Lebanon, under UNSC [United Nations Security Council] 1701.

---

*Reaction to Hamas victory in January 2006 was as firm in Paris as it was in Washington.*

---

## Franco-American Divergences and Convergences Today

Is Nicolas Sarkozy's view of the region very different from that of Jacques Chirac? The two men don't belong to the same generation, and they certainly don't have the same personal ties and experience in the region. In contrast with Chirac's old friendships with many Arab leaders, Nicolas Sarkozy has made clear that he is a friend of Israel—and he is celebrated as such in Tel Aviv and in Washington.

However, a closer look reveals that during the campaign, Nicolas Sarkozy used the same rhetorical device he used vis-à-vis the US, namely "I am a friend of the US/of Israel . . . but real friends tell real friends what they think." And what he thinks does not necessarily coincide with what Americans and/or Israelis would like to hear. For example, he described Israel's war against Hezbollah in the summer of 2006 as "clumsy and disproportionate," the exact code words used by the Quai d'Orsay [French ministry of foreign affairs]. It should be noted, moreover, that starting with the recommendations of a blue-ribbon group of experts in 2002, aggressive steps have been taken under Jacques Chirac to improve Franco-Israeli relations (after all, there are more than 800,000 Francophones in Israel, France is the 6th largest trading partner of Tel Aviv, and people-to-people exchanges are extremely dense), resulting in a marked improvement of diplomatic ties, symbolized by frequent high-level and successful visits of Prime Ministers Sharon then Ehud Olmert in the past two years. Since he took office in May 2007, Nicolas Sarkozy has not noticeably changed France's stance in the region, and has—so far—followed in the footsteps of Jacques Chirac.

So if Sarkozy has not substantially altered French foreign policy, what are the current points of agreement and disagreement between the US and France on the Arab-Israeli conflict?

- At base, there is a strong French-US agreement on the question of security for Israel and condemnation of Palestinian terrorism.

- The convergence on Iran has been remarkable. Nicolas Sarkozy has been vocal in stating that an Iranian nuclear bomb was not acceptable, but Jacques Chirac, before him, had taken a hard line on Iran. This brings the question of the Shia-Sunni rift [Shia and Sunni are Muslim denominations] which has come to dominate the region, whether in Iraq, in Lebanon, or indirectly in the Palestinian territories. On the necessity to contain radical Iranian influence in all of these places, and work with the traditional regional allies, Paris and Washington are in agreement.

- The fate of Lebanon and the adoption of a hard line on Syria was, in 2004, one of the first issues on which France and the US resumed active cooperation, with UNSC resolution 1559 and, in May 2006, resolution 1680.

---

*At base, there is a strong French-US agreement on the question of security for Israel and condemnation of Palestinian terrorism.*

---

## Remaining Differences

There also remain enduring French-US differences.

As mentioned above, Paris is convinced that peace can only come through a process of negotiations between the two enemies, which means that moderate Palestinian leaders such as Mahmoud Abbas should not be sidestepped, and that they should be helped—and not only a few months before the elections, as was seen in the past. Too often in the recent years, Palestinian leaders have been criticized or undercut, especially by the US Congress, and this has been detrimental to the peace process. This rationale is behind France's proposal to host a donors conference in Paris later this year. The conference will be presided over by Tony Blair [British prime minister], the special envoy of the Quartet, who shares this goal of reinforcing Mahmoud Abbas and Prime Minister Salam Fayyad. It is crucial that Mahmoud Abbas be reinforced not only in the donors conference, but in [the Middle East peace conference at] Annapolis as well—a failure to do so would only comfort Hamas, which controls Gaza since June 2007 and is threatening Abbas's rule in the West Bank.

Another aim of the Paris conference is to provide more help to the Palestinian population, who has suffered greatly in recent years, especially in Gaza, where the situation is now close to a humanitarian catastrophe. Paris voices its concern more often than Washington on this issue, and has been providing substantial financial and humanitarian help along with the EU throughout the recent years, because increasing poverty and despair can only lead to further radicalization and embrace of Hamas. Thus for example the Quai d'Orsay reacted negatively on October 29, 2007, when Israeli sanctions against civilians in the Gaza Strip (on electricity and fuel supplies) were tightened.

The Bush administration now advocates the creation of a Palestinian state, while France always insists that it must be a *viable* Palestinian state, not a patchwork of remote pieces of land. France has been much more vocal than Washington about the uninterrupted growth of illegal settlements in occupied territory, especially in East Jerusalem, which will make a final peace agreement more difficult and threaten the viability of the future state. Of particular concern has been the Maale Adounim settlement and the "E1 zone" project, which separates the northern from the southern West Bank. Indeed, on November 18, 2007, while traveling to the region, [French foreign minister] Bernard Kouchner declared that "colonization is not only contrary to law, it is also the main obstacle to peace from a political point of view."

---

*Americans ... tend to think that France is reflexively pro-Palestinian.*

---

The last disagreement has to do with Lebanon. While there is real convergence on this issue, as previously mentioned, France is more concerned with issues of Lebanese domestic politics, while Washington seems more focused on countering Syria there. A good example of this disagreement can be found in the attitude towards Hezbollah, which Washington considers only as a terrorist organization, and which Paris sees also as a political force in Lebanese politics that must be reckoned with. This is why Bernard Kouchner and Nicolas Sarkozy included Hezbollah in the talks at La Celle-Saint-Cloud in July 2007 (aiming at fostering a solution to the political deadlock), a move that triggered an angry letter from the US Congress to Nicolas Sarkozy, authored by Rep. Robert Wexler and signed by 91 of his colleagues. In the recent months, a special advisor to Bernard Kouchner, Jean-Claude Cousseran, and two special representatives of President Sarkozy, Claude Guéant and Jean-David Levitte, were sent to Damascus [Syria] to discuss the coming presidential elections.

A word about perceptions to complete the picture. Enduring stereotypes persist in both countries about the other country's stance on the conflict. For example, the French tend to believe that the US and Israel are always in agreement, while the situation is much more conflictual—it is actually often frustrating, as viewed from Washington. The pro-Israeli lobby is sometimes credited with more influence than it has. Americans, on their part, tend to think that France is reflexively pro-Palestinian, they sometimes distrust French sentiments vis-à-vis the security of Israel, and they ignore the depth and quality of the relationship between Paris and Tel Aviv.

To conclude, there is no doubt that renewed engagement on the part of the Bush administration has been welcomed by Paris and the EU in general, which can more easily associate itself with this policy. As Nicolas Sarkozy said to the US Congress on November 7, 2007: "To the Israeli and Palestinian leaders I say this: Don't hesitate! Risk peace! And do it now! The status quo hides even greater dangers: that of delivering Palestinian society as a whole to the extremists that contest Israel's existence."

# Turkey Has Moved Away from Israel and Toward Syria

## Semih Idiz

*Semih Idiz writes opinion pieces for the* Hürriyet Daily News, *an influential Turkish newspaper. In the following viewpoint, Idiz reports on a conversation with Turkish prime minister Recep Tayyip Erdoğan. Erdoğan emphasized new ties between Turkey and Syria and warned Israel against interfering in the demonstrations against the pro-Western government of Hosni Mubarak in Egypt. Idiz argues that as Egypt moves toward democracy, Israel is becoming more and more isolated and concludes that Israel should try to repair relations with Turkey.*

As you read, consider the following questions:

1. What has made Erdoğan a hero in the eyes of the masses of the Middle East, according to Idiz?
2. Why does Idiz say that Israel's Arab experts missed what was happening in Egypt?
3. What does Idiz say Israel must do to reestablish closer ties with Turkey?

We had the opportunity to fly with [Turkish] Prime Minister [Recep Tayyip] Erdoğan to Hatay [Turkey] and Aleppo [Syria] this weekend [in February 2011] to attend the

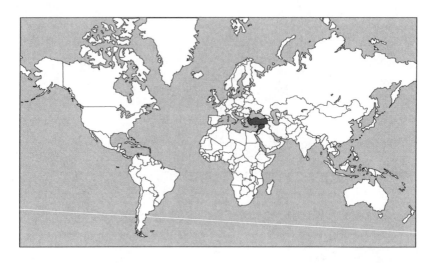

groundbreaking ceremony for the "Friendship Dam" to be built jointly by the two countries [Turkey and Syria] on the historic Asi (Orontes) River.

## Israel's Isolation

No doubt this is going to raise eyebrows in Israel again, given that there is serious unease in that increasingly isolated country over the fast pace of positive developments in Turkish-Syrian ties.

This is of course combined with an increasingly obsessive hatred for Erdoğan among Israelis and Jews across the globe because of his strong and effective support of the Palestinians besieged in Gaza. Israelis have been watching with deep frustration as this stance of Erdoğan has turned him a hero in the eyes of the masses in the Middle East.

Remarks Erdoğan made to us on the plane as we were returning from Syria, however, are bound to increase the animosity felt towards him among Israelis even further. Answering questions for the small group of journalists accompanying him, Erdoğan said—when referring to what must not happen in Egypt [where protests were under way]—that Israel must under no circumstance interfere in that country.

What is more he said that he had underscored the importance of this point in his conversations with [U.S.] President [Barack] Obama and Greek Prime Minister George Papandreou, indicating in this way that they should intervene to stop Israel if it is inclined to meddle in Egypt in a last-ditch effort to try and turn the tide against the anti-[Hosni] Mubarak demonstrators.

It was interesting to note Erdoğan referring to Mr. Papandreou in this context, of course. This could be taken as an indication that Ankara [the capital of Turkey] has already factored into its policy calculations the distinct possibility that Israel and Greece are likely to cozy up to each other in an effort to give the appearance that they are standing together against Turkey.

---

*[There is] an increasingly obsessive hatred for Erdoğan among Israelis and Jews across the globe because of his strong and effective support for the Palestinians besieged in Gaza.*

---

## A State of Panic

Meanwhile the assumption among many regional observers—whether justified or not—is that Israel is in a state of panic over the prospect of losing yet another ally after Turkey and is trying by whatever underhanded means available to ensure that either Hosni Mubarak or a crony or stooge of his stays at the helm of Egypt, instead of the Muslim Brotherhood [an Egyptian Islamic resistance movement] getting hold of it.

But it is more than evident at this stage that this is a futile exercise and that it is unlikely Israel will have its way in this case, given the anti-Mubarak masses that have taken to the streets, among which supporters of the Muslim Brotherhood represent only one element.

As an aside it must be pointed out that for all the "Arabists" Israel is supposed to have and with all its intelligence capabilities, it had no notion of what was brewing in Egypt.

This suggests that these so-called "Arab experts" were more involved in trying to formulate rationalizations for what they wanted to see in that country, rather than focusing on what was really happening there.

---

*Israel is seen as a "destabilizing" factor in the face of the latest developments, just like Iran.*

---

Mr. Erdoğan for his part seems to sense, like many in the region, that if Israel were seen to be interfering in Egypt now, this would be tantamount to throwing a can of petrol on a raging fire. Given that the overall picture shows an Israel which is rapidly losing political ground in the Middle East, some analysts suggest this will make that country "adventurous," and hence "dangerous" in terms of regional stability in the coming period as it tries to influence the course of events.

Put another way, Israel is seen as a "destabilizing" factor in the face of the latest developments, just like Iran, which is trying to manipulate these developments to its own advantage, as seen by the latest remarks from the "chief mullah" in that country on Friday.

Of course one might question justifiably what it is that makes "Turkey's interference" in Egypt "good" while Israel and Iran's interference is "bad." Erdoğan was after all the first one to say in so many words that it was time Mubarak went, a development that gained him a reprimand from the remnants of the Mubarak regime who warned him not to meddle in Egypt.

## Respect for Turkey

On-the-spot coverage by Turkish networks from Tahrir Square and elsewhere in Egypt, however, showed that Erdoğan commands wide respect among the Egyptian people, whatever their oppressive Israeli- and U.S.-supported administrators

## Israel Blocks Gaza-Bound Flotilla, May 31, 2010

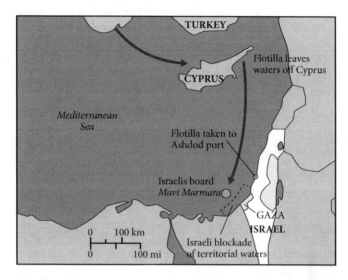

**Flotilla of ships**

- includes the ship *Mavi Marmara*, owned by Islamic Turkish NGO IHH Humanitarian Relief Foundation, two freighters, and three smaller boats

- has more than seven hundred passengers, about 50 percent of whom are Turkish

- carries medicine, food, clothing, and other materials to ease the Israeli blockade of Gaza

- is blocked by Israel in international waters off Gaza on May 31, 2010

- suffers nine fatalities during Israeli blockade attack

- is taken to port of Ashdod after the attack

TAKEN FROM: Yigal Schleifer, "Israeli Raid on Freedom Flotilla Shatters Key Turkey-Israeli Ties," *Christian Science Monitor*, June 1, 2010. www.csmonitor.com.

may say. All the talk among Egyptian analysts and opposition politicians about "the AKP [Justice and Development Party] and the Turkish model," on the other hand, demonstrates the kind of standing Turkey has in the region.

At any rate Erdoğan was quick to point out that Turkey did not intend to interfere actively in Egypt, even if it has opinions about what is happening there, unless, that is, it is called on to provide advice by members of the opposition, and particularly the Muslim Brotherhood—which has become a bogey for the West and Israel.

As to what Turkey wants to see happening in Egypt at this stage, Erdoğan said it was important for that country to hold elections as soon as possible, to amend its constitution to make it more democratic and to modernize its laws on elections and political parties.

While this is not what Israel wants, since it is unlikely that any democratically elected government in Egypt will be as friendly towards Israel as the Mubarak regime has been, it is interesting to note that Washington and Ankara are increasingly on the same page on this score.

On the other hand Erdoğan did tell us that Turkey was prepared to intervene for humanitarian purposes should the systemic breakdown in Egypt result in hunger and disease spreading among the people. Erdoğan said he had instructed the relevant Turkish organizations to ready themselves to send immediate help should such an eventuality come about.

In the meantime he said his government would be calling on an international donors conference for Egypt and would also call on the Security Council to meet urgently to discuss the developments in that country.

---

*The Israeli axe has hit a hard rock this time in confronting Turkey. None of this would have happened ... if ties between the two countries were as they were in the past.*

---

None of this is likely to be pleasing for Israel, while Washington watches with a more open mind given that Erdoğan and his ruling Justice and Development Party, or AKP, can play a moderating role over the Muslim Brotherhood.

Put another way, it is increasingly evident that the Israeli axe has hit a hard rock this time in confronting Turkey. None of this would have happened, of course, if ties between the two countries were as they were in the past.

Whether the latest developments in the region will force Israel to think strategically and apologize to Turkey for killing nine unarmed Turkish pro-Palestinian activist on the *Mavi Marmara* and pay compensation for them—thus paving the way for normalization of ties with Ankara—remains to be seen. [Editor's note: Turkish civilians were killed in May 2010 when a flotilla bearing humanitarian aid to Gaza in violation of an Israeli blockade was boarded by Israeli soldiers.]

While no one is too hopeful on this score it is clear that Israel's, and not Turkey's, quandary is growing.

# In South Africa, Desmond Tutu's Criticism of Israel Has Sparked Controversy

*Melanie Gosling*

*Melanie Gosling is a journalist for the South African* Cape Times. *In the following viewpoint, she reports on the controversy around human rights activist Desmond Tutu. Tutu, she notes, has called for sanctions against Israel because of its human rights record. Supporters of Israel circulated a petition calling Tutu an anti-Semite and demanding he be removed as a trustee of Holocaust centers in South Africa. Gosling also reports on a counterpetition, which calls the charges of anti-Semitism baseless and suggests that Tutu's human rights advocacy makes him an ideal person to serve on the board of the Holocaust institutions.*

As you read, consider the following questions:

1. The petitioners want Tutu to be axed as patron of Holocaust centers in what cities, according to Gosling?
2. What does the petition cite as recent examples of Tutu's "anti-Israel behaviour"?
3. To whom do the lessons of the Holocaust belong, according to the petition supporting Tutu?

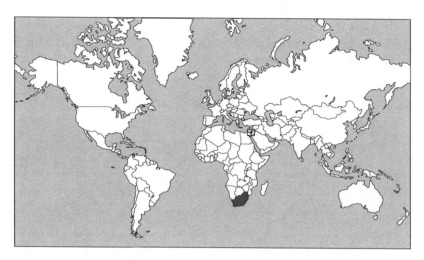

More than 300 people have signed an online petition calling for Nobel Peace laureate Archbishop Emeritus Desmond Tutu to be axed as patron of the Holocaust centres in Cape Town and Johannesburg because of his "numerous anti-Semitic and anti-Israel statements".

The petition, launched by three Capetonians—David Hersch, vice-chairman of the SA Zionist Federation, Joselle Reuben and Howard Joffe—has been signed by 343 people from the UK, US, New Zealand, Germany, Canada and South Africa, all of whom support the call for the trustees of both centres to give Tutu the boot.

The petition describes Tutu's call to stop the Cape Town Opera Company from performing in Israel late in 2010, and for academic institutions to cut ties with those in Israel, as "only the most recent examples of Archbishop Tutu's anti-Israel behaviour".

It describes Tutu's support for sanctions against Israel as "morally repugnant" based on "horrific and grotesquely false accusation against the Jewish people".

Hersch and other signatories called on the trustees of the Cape Town Holocaust Centre and the Johannesburg Holocaust & Genocide Centre to "have the courage to avoid the politically correct and cowardly route . . . and terminate Archbishop Tutu's patronage of both Holocaust centres in South Africa".

---

*[The petition] describes Tutu's support for sanctions against Israel as "morally repugnant" based on "horrific and grotesquely false accusation against the Jewish people".*

---

The petition said no matter what honours had been earned by Tutu, he was not above sanction.

"His track record regarding Israel and his many anti-Israel pronouncements speak volumes as to his being the wrong person to hold this position," it said.

A paragraph at the end calls on the trustees also to terminate the appointments of Professor Kader Asmal and Judge Richard Goldstone as patrons of the Holocaust centres. The petition was picked up by Harvard law professor Alan Dershowitz, who wrote an online article in *FrontPage Magazine* called "Tutu and the Jews", in which he states: "The decent people of South Africa have become aware of Tutu's bigotry. . . . It is time for the rest of the world to recognise that the bishop is no saint.

"When it comes to Jews, he is an unrepentant sinner".

Dershowitz, a frequent commentator on the Israel/Arab conflict, is known for his involvement in several celebrity court cases, including those of Mike Tyson, Patty Hearst and OJ Simpson.

One of the comments below Dershowitz's article, signed by "Johnny", states: "Chain Tutu to a plough and let him pick some taters."

Now another group of South Africans has launched a counter online petition in defence of Tutu, calling him "the most appropriate patron of the South African Holocaust foundation".

The pro-Tutu petition has been signed by 381 people from several countries.

South Africans who have signed it include Arthur Chaskalson, former head of the Constitutional Court and now president of the International Commission of Jurists, human rights lawyer Geoff Budlender and Nathan Geffen of the Treatment Action Campaign.

The petition states that while the Holocaust was a crime against humanity that must never be forgotten, its lessons belonged to "all of humanity".

The mission of the Holocaust foundation was to build "a more caring and just society in which human rights and diversity are respected and valued".

"This is precisely the cause to which Tutu has dedicated his life. He represents the finest tradition of resistance to all forms of oppression. To call him an anti-Semite because he has attacked the policies of the Israeli government is outrageous, renders the term meaningless, and enfeebles the necessary efforts to defeat real anti-Semites and racists," the petition says.

Tutu's life had been lived in the spirit of "never again", which was the ultimate lesson of the Holocaust.

---

*"To call him an anti-Semite because he has attacked the policies of the Israeli government is outrageous ... and enfeebles the necessary efforts to defeat real anti-Semites and racists."*

---

While disagreements should be debated openly, to call Tutu an anti-Semite and a bigot were personal attacks and totally unacceptable.

"We, the undersigned, give our support to Archbishop Emeritus Desmond Tutu as a most appropriate patron of the South African Holocaust foundation," the petition said.

## Tutu in Palestine

On Christmas Eve [1989], Tutu went to preach at Shepherds' Field near Bethlehem, which lay outside Beit Sahour, a mostly Christian town under siege by the Israeli army. Disembarking from their cars, Tutu, [Michael] Nuttall [a long-time Tutu assistant], and [Palestinian Bishop Samir] Kafity were mobbed by thousands of Palestinians. Defying the Israelis, members of the crowd waved olive branches and chanted, "ANC [African National Congress, the ruling party of post-apartheid South Africa], PLO [Palestine Liberation Organization]," "PLO, Israel No." Women held up signs reading, "No to racism and occupation; yes to democracy and independence." Carols and readings from the New Testament were interspersed with the exuberant responses of an impromptu political rally. To applause, shouts, and whistling, Tutu stated his support of Palestinian nationhood. "But," he added, "we say also, dear brothers and sisters, the Jews have a right to their independent state as well."

*John Allen,*
Rabble-Rouser for Peace:
The Authorized Biography of Desmond Tutu.
*Chicago, IL: Chicago Review Press, 2006, p. 386.*

A comment by signatory Rebecca Elfasi of the UK states: "How can anyone who established the Truth and Reconciliation Commission in South Africa, and is a beacon of light around the world for truth, humanity and goodness, be accused of something so vile? He is one of the greatest human beings of all time."

Tutu, who is in Zurich where he was given the FIFA Presidential Award for 2010 on Monday, was not available for comment.

Richard Freedman, the director of the Cape Town Holocaust Centre, and its chairman, Mervyn Smith, also overseas, could not be reached for comment.

However, Freedman's assistant, Jurina de Jager, said on Tuesday: "The response I received is that our office and Tutu's office will deal with the matter of the petition together when they all get back."

# Oil Embargoes Probably Cannot Be Used to Influence US Policy on the Arab-Israeli Conflict

## Robert Mabro

*Robert Mabro is an emeritus fellow at St Antony's College and a fellow at St Catherine's College, Oxford University; he is the author of* Oil in the Twentieth Century. *In the following viewpoint, he argues that the Arab oil embargo in 1973–74 was not an effective weapon against the West. Mabro adds that a similar embargo would be even less effective now. However, the uncertainties of the Arab-Israeli conflict and the West's reliance on oil mean that oil disruptions are possible. Mabro says that the best short-term solution to this problem is for nations to build strategic oil supplies, as the United States has done.*

As you read, consider the following questions:

1. What does Mabro say was the first phase of the "oil price shock"?

2. According to Mabro, how long did the effective use of the oil weapon last?

3. What does Mabro believe would have to happen before Hugo Chávez of Venezuela would restrict oil exports to the United States?

Robert Mabro, "The Oil Weapon—Can It Be Used Today?," *The Harvard International Review*, December 31, 2007. Copyright © 2007 *The Harvard International Review*. Reproduced with permission.

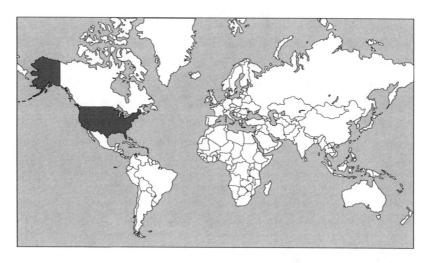

In 1973 the Arab oil-exporting countries stunned the world by announcing that they were cutting oil production and placing an oil embargo on the United States and the Netherlands. Now, 35 years later, fears about the security of oil supplies are provoking concern that Iran or a similarly hostile country might have recourse to some form of the oil weapon again. However, upon examination of the historical precedent—the use of the oil weapon in 1973 and 1974—it becomes clear that the oil weapon is a blunt instrument that cannot be applied in a focused manner for any sustained period.

## The Oil Weapon of 1973–1974

On October 16, 1973, an OPEC [Organization of the Petroleum Exporting Countries] committee consisting of the oil ministers of the six Gulf member countries (United Arab Emirates, Iran, Iraq, Kuwait, Qatar, and Saudi Arabia) announced that they would unilaterally increase the posted price of Arabian Light, the marker crude, from US$3.011 per barrel to US$5.119—an increase of 70 percent. This price decision was the first phase of what became known in the developed world as the "oil price shock."

The next day, the five Arab members of the OPEC committee were joined in Kuwait by the oil ministers of Algeria, Bahrain, Egypt, Libya, and Syria. Although the meeting included all the members of the Organization of Arab Petroleum Exporting Countries (OAPEC), it was not convened as an OAPEC Council of Ministers, but rather as a Conference of Arab Oil Ministers. Indeed, the purpose of the meeting was political rather than economic and fell outside the OAPEC remit. The ministers were trying to agree on how to use the oil weapon to persuade the United States to reconsider its "blind and unlimited support for Israel" and to force the evacuation of occupied territories.

The October, Yom Kippur, or Ramadan War (which, like the English Channel, has different names depending on which side of the divide one stands) had begun on October 6, 1973. But Arab frustrations with the Israeli refusal to evacuate occupied territories and implement a number of UN [United Nations] resolutions had been deepening even before the war. These frustrations had been aggravated on a number of occasions by perceptions that the United States was perpetually standing behind Israel in total indifference to the Arab plight. The idea that an oil weapon might be used to shake US indifference was introduced in 1971 and 1972, and King Faisal of Saudi Arabia went so far as to issue a warning in a meeting held with top executives of the Aramco parent companies (Exxon, SoCal, Texaco, and Mobil) in Geneva on May 23, 1973. The message was that the United States might "lose everything" unless it changed its policy toward the Arab-Israeli conflict. The possibility of a cutback in oil production was mentioned again in subsequent press interviews.

The meeting of the ten Arab oil ministers in Kuwait on October 17 produced, with remarkable speed, a resolution detailing the steps to be taken. Nine countries signed the resolution. Iraq was the only one to decline, as it strongly preferred the nationalization of oil concessions to the use of the oil weapon.

At this meeting, it was determined that the oil weapon would be deployed as follows: The nine signatory countries would reduce their oil production forthwith by at least 5 percent from the actual September 1973 levels, "with a similar reduction to be applied each successive month, computed on the basis of the previous month's production." Care would also be taken to ensure that friendly states would not be affected by the reduction. The production cuts would continue until Israel evacuated the occupied territories and the legitimate rights of the Palestinian people were restored.

---

*The message [in 1973] was that the United States might "lose everything" unless it changed its policy toward the Arab-Israeli conflict.*

---

The decision on the production cut was then modified on November 4. Production cuts were raised to 25 percent below the September level, to be implemented in November. This was to be followed by a further 5 percent reduction in December. The different categories of oil-consuming states were finally set as follows. First, most favored countries would receive their full requirement of oil. Second, preferred countries would be allowed to import "the equivalent of their average imports of Arab oil during the first nine months of 1973 or during the month of September 1973, whichever was greater." Third, neutral countries' imports would be reduced by the same rate as the general cutback and by a proportion of the additional amounts supplied to the most favored and preferred countries. Fourth, embargoed countries would receive no supply of Arab oil. These countries included the United States, the Netherlands, Portugal, South Africa, and Rhodesia.

## Not a Successful Policy

It is immediately clear that such a scheme would be difficult to implement. To cut oil production by a certain percentage is one thing; to reallocate the remaining supplies to importing countries according to four different groupings and a number of criteria is something else altogether. Furthermore, the across-the-board production cuts would cause world oil prices to rise. Indeed this is exactly what happened. The economies of both friends and foes among oil-importing countries were affected. Indeed, the paradox was that friendly oil-importing developing countries were likely to suffer more adverse economic impacts than did the rich industrialized states targeted as foes. In this respect, the oil weapon was—and remains—a very blunt instrument.

Diplomatic pressures and the realization of exaggerated expectations about US willingness and ability to act effectively toward a resolution of the 25-year-old Arab-Israeli conflict began to weaken Arab resolve as early as December 1973. Already at a meeting held in Kuwait on November 19, 1973, the Arab oil ministers had begun to show that they were open to flexibility. They decided not to impose the 5 percent supply reduction scheduled for December on European Economic Community countries (other than the Netherlands) in appreciation of some friendly statements made by the Europeans. A week later Japan and the Philippines, both deemed to be friendly, were exempted.

---

*The oil weapon was—and remains—a very blunt instrument.*

---

The notion that the oil weapon was an "instrument of flexible persuasion" turned out to be little more than public relations spin. On December 24 and 25, the 25 percent production cutback rate from the September levels was reduced to 15 percent, and the 5 percent reduction scheduled for January 1974 was abandoned. Meanwhile, Egyptian President Anwar Sadat, who had placed great hopes in his "friend Henry," as he used to refer to US Secretary of State Henry Kissinger, was persuaded that the lifting of the embargo on the United States would enable US diplomacy to begin working toward the desired goal of the evacuation of occupied territories. President Sadat then made great efforts to convince King Faisal of Saudi Arabia, the leader of the oil weapon initiative, of the merits of lifting the embargo.

Sadat eventually succeeded. At a meeting in Vienna on March 18, 1974, the Arab oil ministers decided to lift the embargo on the United States. For all intents and purposes, the oil weapon was abandoned when the embargo on the United States was abandoned. The use of the oil weapon had lasted for almost five months. Yet because a number of successive relaxations increased oil supplies to the world economy, it could reasonably be said that the effective use of the weapon did not last for more than three months.

## Lessons for Today

This analysis of the only serious instance of the use of an oil weapon by oil-exporting countries reveals the difficulties that a developing state would likely face if it attempted to wield this instrument in the context of a political dispute with the United States or another OECD [Organisation for Economic Co-operation and Development] country.

The oil weapon is a blunt instrument. The international oil trade involves a large number of exporting countries, and there are many more today than there were in 1973. An embargo imposed on one or a few importers will not necessarily deprive these states of access to oil supplies, so long as other sources remain available. Indeed, the embargo would need to be associated with a very significant cut in oil production to ensure that the embargoed country would not be able to satisfy its demand for oil.

Despite fears about Iran or Venezuela, a significant cut in world oil supplies cannot be achieved by a single oil-exporting country. Saudi Arabia is the only producer that has the necessary weight to do so, but today it is the least likely country to resort to using the oil weapon.

A production cut, if implemented in a tight market, would cause prices to rise and adversely affect all importing countries. Friendly states that are so affected would plead with the countries wielding the oil weapon to relax the measures or grant them exceptional treatment. And if these requests were to be even partially satisfied, the whole system would begin to unravel, as occurred in 1973 and 1974.

---

*Despite fears about Iran and Venezuela, a significant cut in world oil supplies cannot be achieved by a single oil-exporting country.*

---

The embargoed countries, if endowed with military power as well as economic and political clout, would begin to threaten those that were imposing the sanctions. In 1973 and 1974, Kissinger and [historian and critic Arthur] Schlesinger [Jr.] hinted at the possible use of military intervention on a number of occasions. This did not happen, perhaps because the Soviet Union was seen as a constraint on the United States' ability to use military force, or perhaps because Kissinger was too wise to risk offensive action in an explosive and complex Middle East. But there is no countervailing force like the Soviet Union today, and the global balance of power that has so far marked the 21st century is radically different from that which existed in the early 1970s.

## Panic and Vulnerability

There is no doubt that the use of the oil weapon in October 1973 caused a panic among oil-importing states. These countries quickly became conscious of their vulnerability as they recognized their dependency on non-substitutable oil for critical uses (both in the transport sector and in other sectors, in which fuel substitution was technically possible but could not be achieved in the short term). There was also a sense of outrage among OECD states. How could a group of weak, developing countries challenge the world's great powers with such initial success? The perception was that the economic balance of power had shifted, thanks to the monopoly [that] was enjoyed by the OPEC countries.

But the way in which the use of the oil weapon was gradually relaxed after its early escalation in November 1973 tells a different story. The oil-exporting countries were, in fact, quite weak. Having failed to achieve their political objectives, they abandoned the US embargo. After 35 years, Israel is still occupying land seized in 1967, and the Arab-Israeli conflict is still plaguing the Middle East.

---

*How could a group of weak, developing countries challenge the world's great powers with such initial success?*

---

As developing countries, potential aggressors are conscious that they are both dependent and vulnerable. They rely on the outside world for vital supplies, from food to pharmaceutical products, and for both consumer and capital goods. Their recent wealth in the form of foreign exchange reserves leaves them dependent on the international financial system. There is, to say the least, mutual dependence between the oil exporters and the rich industrialized countries. Although the latter's dependence is based on a single good—oil—the former are dependent on a variety of goods and services imported from abroad.

Subsequent historical developments further revealed that the balance of power at that time favored the West. Indeed, the direction of oil weapon use was actually reversed, as the United Nations and United States used oil sanctions against Libya, Iraq, and Iran. Moreover, unlike the OPEC's effort of 1973, these embargoes were not short stints of three to six months, but rather lasted for a number of years. The experience of 1973—the first and last use of the oil weapon by oil-exporting countries—clearly shows that it is not easy (or perhaps possible at all) to achieve political objectives with this instrument.

The deterrent today against the use of the oil weapon by one or more Gulf countries is the significant US military presence in the region. The United States has bases in Kuwait, Qatar, Bahrain, Iraq, and Kyrgyzstan and a sizeable US naval force sails in the waters of the Gulf. This was not the case, at least to the same extent, in 1973, as the Cold War restricted the military activities of the two existing superpowers.

## Iran and Venezuela

Iran might initially retaliate if it were attacked by the United States, Israel, or some coalition thereof. It could reduce the volume of its oil exports. The loss of one million barrels a day would initially push prices up. Yet a shortfall of one million barrels a day could be easily compensated for by a release of oil from strategic stocks held in the United States, Europe, and Japan, and by the use of surge capacity in producing countries. In addition, it is difficult to identify oil-exporting countries that might join Iran in wielding the oil weapon.

Some lurid scenarios involving Iranian attacks against oil installations in other Gulf countries or attempts to close the Straits of Hormuz have engendered a certain amount of fear. But they lack credibility, as they ignore the existence of a powerful US deterrent in the region.

President [Hugo] Chávez of Venezuela is just as unlikely to use the oil weapon. Despite a series of threats to restrict oil exports to the United States, Chávez would most likely never take such a risk unless there is a US-backed attempt to overthrow his regime, or if Venezuela is subjected to a US military attack—which is highly improbable. Since the volume of Venezuelan oil exports to the United States is large (some 1.5 million barrels per day), any sustained interruption could cause significant disturbances to the world oil market and the domestic Venezuelan economy.

Markets react very nervously to more benign events than this. The release of such a volume from the US strategic stockpile would lead politicians or the media to question the wisdom of depleting oil reserves at that rate over a long period of time. The International Atomic Energy Agency would be called into action, but the performance of this institution in the crises of 1979 and 1990 with the use of its "safety net" did not inspire much optimism.

---

*This is not to say that the use of the oil weapon cannot or will not be launched. The implication of this analysis is simply that if launched, it could not be sustained.*

---

Even if oil prices did rise significantly, Venezuela's oil revenues would inevitably suffer, simply because the volume of Venezuelan oil exports to the United States is a large proportion of the country's total exports. A 75 percent reduction in exports calls for an impossible fourfold increase in prices to keep revenues constant. In such a situation, Venezuela would certainly find the revenue loss simply unsustainable.

This is not to say that the use of the oil weapon cannot or will not be launched. The implication of this analysis is simply that if launched, it could not be sustained. It is clear that the attempted use of the oil weapon by Iran or Venezuela, or any extremist regime in an oil-exporting country, bears a relationship to aggressive policies pursued by the United States. Thus, a radical change in Western policies toward the Middle East and developing countries in general may improve the security situation in the long run.

## The Energy Security Issue

Worries about the potential use of the oil weapon are part of a multifarious concern about the security of oil supplies. This supply could be similarly affected by technical accidents; storms; terrorist attacks on oil facilities; civil unrest in oil-producing provinces of exporting countries; failures to invest at an appropriate rate in exploration, development, or production; and the premature arrival of a production peak. Given all these potentialities, the oil weapon should not be the only, or even the primary, concern—for, as argued above, even if it is launched, it cannot be sustained.

The United States, the European Union, and Japan all want to reduce dependence on oil for both security and environmental reasons. The means that have been proposed are twofold: fuel substitution in favor of nuclear, renewable energy, gas, or coal, and more efficient energy use. Some progress has been achieved on both fronts. But the reductions required to mitigate the world's reliance on oil from Iran, Venezuela, and other unstable states are beyond what can be obtained in the short or medium term. A reduction of dependence on oil imports in the United States, Europe, and Japan is unattainable for the simple reason that a country importing 12 million barrels per day (the United States) would not be less vulnerable to a supply problem if it managed to reduce its import volume to 9 or 10 million barrels per day. Only a technical revolution in the fueling of automobile engines could kill the thirst for oil in these countries, and this may not happen for at least 20 years.

---

*The policy that makes the most sense for the short and medium run is the development of a strategic oil stockpile.*

---

In any case, there is a dependence paradox: Reducing oil import volume does not reduce vulnerability to an oil supply shock, so long as these volumes remain somewhat significant.

The implications of this analysis may provide some comfort on one very important point: The likelihood of the oil weapon being used outside a war launched against Iran by the United States is very small. And even in that case, the implementation of the oil weapon cannot be sustained. But the overall security of oil supplies, as mentioned above, is threatened by a host of factors and potential events.

Although a wide range of policies must be pursued for long-term energy security considerations, the policy that makes the most sense for the short and medium run is the development of a strategic oil stockpile. The reason is simply that a supply shortfall, caused by any number of potential developments, could then be easily compensated for by releasing oil from this stockpile. This has been achieved to a certain extent in Japan. The volume currently stocked by the United States is probably close to the optimum amount, though this judgment may differ among experts with different degrees of risk aversion. However, strategic stockpiling must be associated with the design and publication of clear procedures for its use in different types of emergencies. Uncertainty in this context can deprive the strategic stockpile of its utility.

# Periodical and Internet Sources Bibliography

*The following articles have been selected to supplement the diverse views presented in this chapter.*

| | |
|---|---|
| Conrad Black | "Israel's Friends in Canada," *Full Comment* (blog), June 11, 2010. http://fullcomment .nationalpost.com. |
| Beril Dedeoglu | "Turkey, Israel and the First Step," *Today's Zaman*, March 19, 2011. |
| Foreign Affairs and International Trade Canada | "Canadian Policy on Key Issues in the Israeli-Palestinian Conflict," August 18, 2011. www .international.gc.ca. |
| France 24 | "Valérie Hoffenberg, France's Envoy to the Middle East Peace Process," August 2, 2011. www.france24.com. |
| Warren Goldstein | "An Open Letter to Tutu," *Jerusalem Post*, November 3, 2010. |
| *Hindu* | "India Backs Arab Peace Initiative," March 1, 2010. |
| Tony Long | "Oct. 17, 1973: Angry Arabs Turn Off the Oil Spigot," *Wired*, October 17, 2008. |
| Reuters | "France Wants Middle-East Peace Talks Kick-Start: PM," February 21, 2010. www.reuters .com. |
| Yigal Schleifer | "Why Israel Humiliated Turkey in Response to a TV Show," *Christian Science Monitor*, January 12, 2010. |
| Philip Stephens | "Europe's Stand on Middle East Peace," *Financial Times*, March 17, 2011. |
| Hasan Suroor | "Indian Support for UN Resolution on Israel Angered U.S.," *Hindu*, March 25, 2011. |

# For Further Discussion

## Chapter 1

1. David M. Weinberg says that Iran is the real threat to the Middle East, not Israel; Yousef Munayyer says Israel is the threat, not Iran. Which do you feel has the better argument? Could Israel and Iran both be destabilizing forces, or can it be only one or the other? Explain.

2. Based on the viewpoint by the Carnegie Endowment for International Peace, will water necessarily be a source of cooperation in the Middle East? What other effect might dwindling water resources have on the region?

## Chapter 2

1. Based on the viewpoints from Martin Bright and Johann Hari, do you think that negotiating with terrorists is helpful or harmful? Would Israel negotiating with Hamas be similar to the United States negotiating with a terrorist organization such as al Qaeda? Explain your answer.

2. Does Daud Abdullah ever show that Israel did intentionally target civilians in the Gaza war, or that Hamas did not? Is this issue important for his argument or not?

## Chapter 3

1. Of the authors in this chapter, which seem to believe that working toward peace in the Middle East is a worthwhile or feasible goal? Which do not? Explain your answer.

2. Amnesty International argues that the restrictions on Palestinian movement are too harsh; Hila Tene of the Israeli government says they are not too harsh. Is a human rights

agency more likely to be objective on this issue, or is the Israeli government in a better position to evaluate the issue? Explain your answer.

## Chapter 4

1. There are many areas of conflict in the world. Based on the viewpoints in this chapter, why is the Arab-Israeli conflict of such importance to so many other nations?

2. Does Semih Idiz seem skeptical of the Turkish leader Recep Tayyip Erdoğan, or does he support him? How might this attitude impact reporting on the Arab-Israeli conflict?

# Organizations to Contact

*The editors have compiled the following list of organizations concerned with the issues debated in this book. The descriptions are derived from materials provided by the organizations. All have publications or information available for interested readers. The list was compiled on the date of publication of the present volume; the information provided here may change. Be aware that many organizations take several weeks or longer to respond to inquiries, so allow as much time as possible.*

**American Jewish Committee (AJC)**
PO Box 705, New York, NY   10150
(212) 751-4000
e-mail: pr@ajc.org
website: www.ajc.org

The American Jewish Committee (AJC) is an international think tank and pro-Israel advocacy organization that works to strengthen US-Israeli relations, build international support for Israel, and support the Israeli-Arab peace process. AJC's website contains links to breaking news stories; opinion surveys; and a wealth of AJC articles and publications, including for example, the report "Syria: Brokering Hate on Israel's Border" and "AJC Mideast Briefing: The Second Gaza Flotilla."

**Americans for Middle East Understanding (AMEU)**
475 Riverside Drive, Room 245, New York, NY   10115-0245
(212) 870-2053 • fax: (212) 870-2050
e-mail: info@ameu.org
website: www.ameu.org

Americans for Middle East Understanding (AMEU) is an organization founded to foster a better understanding in America of the history, goals, and values of Middle Eastern cultures and peoples; the rights of Palestinians; and the forces shaping US policy in the Middle East. AMEU publishes *The Link*, a bimonthly newsletter, as well as books and pamphlets on the Middle East.

### Begin-Sadat Center for Strategic Studies (BESA)

Bar-Ilan University, Ramat Gan   52900
  Israel
972-3-535-9198 • fax: 972-3-535-9195
e-mail: besa.center@mail.biu.ac.il
website: http://www.biu.ac.il/Besa/

The Begin-Sadat Center for Strategic Studies (BESA) seeks to contribute to the advancement of Middle East peace and security, especially as it relates to the national security and foreign policy of Israel, by conducting policy-relevant research on strategic subjects. It publishes monographs and periodical series, as well as frequent papers and a biannual news bulletin. Papers and bulletins are available through its website.

### Council on Foreign Relations (CFR)

58 E. Sixty-Eighth Street, New York, NY   10065
(212) 434-9400 • fax: (212) 434-9800
e-mail: communications@cfr.org
website: www.cfr.org

The Council on Foreign Relations (CFR) researches the international aspects of American economic and political policies. Its journal, *Foreign Affairs*, published five times a year, provides analysis on global conflicts. Articles on its website include "Israel, the Bomb, and Openness" and "Crisis-Guide: The Israeli-Palestinian Conflict."

### Foundation for Middle East Peace (FMEP)

1761 N Street NW, Washington, DC   20036
(202) 835-3650 • fax: (202) 835-3651
e-mail: info@fmep.org
website: www.fmep.org

The Foundation for Middle East Peace (MFEP) is a nonprofit organization that promotes a peaceful resolution of the Israeli-Palestinian conflict. To do this, it sponsors programs and public speaking events, makes small financial grants, and publishes the bimonthly *Report on Israeli Settlements in the Occupied Territories*, which contains analysis and commentary on the Arab-Israeli conflict.

### Institute for Palestine Studies (IPS)
3501 M Street NW, Washington, DC   20007
(202) 342-3990 • fax: (202) 342-3927
e-mail: ipsdc@palestine-studies.org
website: www.palestine-studies.org

Institute for Palestine Studies (IPS) is a nonprofit, pro-Arab institute unaffiliated with any political organization or government. Established in 1963 in Beirut, the institute promotes research, analysis, and documentation of the Arab-Israeli conflict and its resolution. IPS publishes quarterlies in three languages and maintains offices all over the world. The institute's US branch publishes four quarterly journals in three languages, including the *Journal of Palestinian Studies* and the *Jerusalem Quarterly*, as well as numerous books and articles on the Arab-Israeli conflict and Palestinian affairs.

### Israel Ministry of Foreign Affairs
9 Yitzhak Rabin Boulevard, Jerusalem   91950
972-2-5303111 • fax: 972-2-5303367
e-mail: sar@mfa.gov.il
website: www.mfa.gov.il/MFA

The Israeli Ministry of Foreign Affairs is the Israeli cabinet-level department responsible for international relations. Its website includes news reports, policy statements, speeches, treaties, and other information relating to Israel's relations with its neighbors.

### Jordan Information Bureau
3504 International Drive NW, Washington, DC   20008
(202) 265-1606 • fax: (202) 667-0777
e-mail: JordanInfo@aol.com
website: www.jordanembassyus.org/new/jib/indexjib.shtml

The Jordan Information Bureau provides political, cultural, and economic information on Jordan. It publishes fact sheets, speeches by Jordanian officials, and government documents, many of which are available on its website.

## Middle East Institute

1761 N Street NW, Washington, DC  20036-2882
(202) 785-1141 • fax: (202) 331-8861
e-mail: mideasti@mideasti.org
website: www.mideasti.org

The Middle East Institute's mission is to promote better understanding of Middle Eastern cultures, languages, religions, and politics. It publishes numerous books, papers, audiotapes, and videos, as well as the quarterly *Middle East Journal.*

## Middle East Media Research Institute (MEMRI)

PO Box 27837, Washington, DC  20038-7837
(202) 955-9070 • fax: (202) 955-9077
e-mail: memri@memri.org
website: www.memri.org

The Middle East Media Research Institute (MEMRI) is a nonprofit, nonpartisan organization that translates and disseminates articles and commentaries from Middle East media sources and provides analysis on the political, ideological, intellectual, social, cultural, and religious trends in the region.

## Muslim Council of Britain (MCB)

PO Box 57330, London  E1 2WJ
+44 (0) 845 26 26 786 • fax: +44 (0) 207 247 7079
e-mail:admin@mcb.org.uk
website: www.mcb.org.uk/index.php

The Muslim Council of Britain (MCB) is a national British representative Muslim umbrella body with more than five hundred affiliated national, regional, and local organizations, mosques, charities, and schools. It works to promote a just position for Muslims within British society. Its website includes many articles on Middle Eastern affairs, including "How to Help the People of Gaza" and "Gaza Today, Jerusalem Tomorrow."

# Bibliography of Books

| | |
|---|---|
| John Ankerberg and Dillon Burroughs | *Middle East Meltdown: Oil, Israel, and the Religion Behind the Crisis.* Eugene, OR: Harvest House Publishers, 2007. |
| Ian J. Bickerton and Carla L. Klausner | *A History of the Arab-Israeli Conflict.* 6th ed. Boston, MA: Prentice Hall, 2010. |
| Charles L. Campbell | *On a Clear Day I Can See Armageddon: The Collision of Israel, Islam, and Oil.* Tucson, AZ: Fenestra Books, 2003. |
| Anthony H. Cordesman, Aram Nerguizian, and Inout C. Popescu | *Israel and Syria: The Military Balance and Prospects of War.* Westport, CT: Praeger Security International, 2008. |
| Jerome R. Corsi | *Why Israel Can't Wait: The Coming War Between Israel and Iran.* New York: Simon & Schuster, 2009. |
| Elisha Efrat | *The West Bank and Gaza Strip: A Geography of Occupation and Dissent.* New York: Routledge, 2005. |
| Caroline B. Glick | *Shackled Warrior: Israel and the Global Jihad.* New York: Geffen, 2008. |
| Gershom Gorenberg | *The Accidental Empire: Israel and the Birth of the Settlements, 1967–1977.* New York: Times Books, 2006. |

Adam Horowitz, Lizzy Ratner, and Philip Weiss, eds. *The Goldstone Report: The Legacy of the Landmark Investigation of the Gaza Conflict.* New York: Nation Books, 2011.

Ann Mosely Lesch and Mark Tessler *Israel, Egypt, and the Palestinians: From Camp David to Intifada.* Bloomington, IN: Indiana University Press, 1989.

Matthew Levitt *Hamas: Politics, Charity, and Terrorism in the Service of Jihad.* New Haven, CT: Yale University Press, 2006.

Gideon Levy *The Punishment of Gaza.* New York: Verso, 2010.

Giulio Meotti *A New Shoah: The Untold Story of Israel's Victims of Terrorism.* New York: Encounter Books, 2010.

Augustus Richard Norton *Hezbollah: A Short History.* Princeton, NJ: Princeton University Press, 2007.

Trita Parsi *Treacherous Alliance: The Secret Dealings of Israel, Iran, and the United States.* New Haven, CT: Yale University Press, 2008.

Nigel Parsons *The Politics of the Palestinian Authority: From Oslo to al-Aqsa.* New York: Routledge, 2005.

Walid Phares *The Coming Revolution: Struggle for Freedom in the Middle East.* New York: Threshold Editions, 2010.

Steven W. Popper
et al.
*Natural Gas and Israel's Energy Future: Near-Term Decisions from a Strategic Perspective.* Santa Monica, CA: RAND, 2009.

Jonathan Schneer
*The Balfour Declaration: The Origins of the Arab-Israeli Conflict.* New York: Random House, 2010.

Jan Selby
*Water, Power and Politics in the Middle East: The Other Israeli-Palestinian Conflict.* New York: I.B. Tauris & Co., 2003.

Hillel Shuval and
Hassan Dweik,
eds.
*Water Resources in the Middle East: Israel-Palestinian Water Issues—From Conflict to Cooperation.* Berlin, Germany: Springer-Verlag, 2010.

Asher Susser
*Israel, Jordan, and Palestine: The Two-State Imperative.* Waltham, MA: Brandeis University Press, 2011.

Michael J. Totten
*The Road to Fatima Gate: The Beirut Spring, the Rise of Hezbollah, and the Iranian War Against Israel.* New York: Encounter Books, 2011.

Philip C. Winslow
*Victory for Us Is to See You Suffer: In the West Bank with the Palestinians and the Israelis.* Boston, MA: Beacon Press, 2007.

Idith Zertal and
Akiva Eldar
*Lords of the Land: The War over Israel's Settlement in the Occupied Territories.* Philadelphia, PA: Nation Books, 2007.

# Index

# P

Israeli attack on nuclear
power plant, 42–53
Lebanon relations, 44–45, 173
oil embargo, 190–195
peace efforts, 23
political change may isolate
Israel, 21
Turkey has moved toward,
175–181
unrest has divided opinion in
Golan Heights, 26–29
U.S. relations, 43, 49, 51, 172
water as a cooperative force,
55–59

**T**

Tene, Helen, 130–138
Terrorism
France and U.S. condemna-
tion, 171
Hamas is a dangerous terror-
ist organization, 67–72, 170
Hezbollah, 173
justifies restrictions on West
Bank movements, 131–138
al Qaeda, 168
Syria, 51
Texaco, 190
Toameh, Kaled Abu, 110–111
Topol, Sarah A., 14
Trade
China and Israel, 15
E.U. and Israel, 153
Travel bans. *See* Movement restric-
tions
Tripartite Aggression. *See* Suez
Crisis
**Turkey, 175–181**
Egypt relations, 176–180
flotilla raid, 101, 104–105,
108, 179

has moved from Israel toward
Syria, 175–181
Iran relations, 34
water as a cooperative force,
55–59
Tutu, Desmond, 182–187
Two-state solution
E.U. support, 158
Fayyad plan, 147–149
Netanyahu's acceptance, 110
recognition of Israel and, 157
U.S. and France support, 173
*See also* Statehood, Palestin-
ian; Statehood, recognition
of Israel's

**U**

Unemployment, 96–97
UNHRC (United Nations Human
Rights Council), 81–85, 86–89
UNIFIL, 157, 170
United Arab Emirates oil em-
bargo, 189–195
United Kingdom
Gaza War (2008-2009), 69–72
Islamism, 71–72
Mau Mau Rebellion lawsuit,
88
Suez Crisis, 92
universal jurisdiction and war
crimes, 93
United Nations
blockade monitoring, 96, 128–
129
Gaza War, 81–85, 86–89
Lebanon force and borders,
157–158, 170, 172
oil sanctions, 195–196
peace negotiations role, 157
settlements, 89
water rights, 56